FILM & TV PLACES OF WALES

FILM & TV PLACES OF WALES

CELYN JONES
& FRANCES TURPIN

SEREN

Seren Books is the book imprint of
Poetry Wales Press Ltd
Derwen Road, Bridgend, Wales

www.serenbooks.com
Find us on social media @SerenBooks

Edited by Tracey Rhys

ISBN 978-1-78172-792-8

A CIP record for this title is available from the British Library.

The publisher works with the financial assistance of the Books Council of Wales.

EU GPSR Authorised Representative
Logos Europe, 9 rue Nicolas Poussin, 17000,
La Rochelle, France
E-mail: Contact@logoseurope.eu

Cover photograph: Filming of 'The Toll' in Pembrokeshire, courtesy of Andrew Ryan Hooper
Backcover photograph: Behind-the-scenes filming of 'Snow White & the Huntsman', taken by Penny Skuse

Printed by 4Edge Ltd, Hockley.

CONTENTS

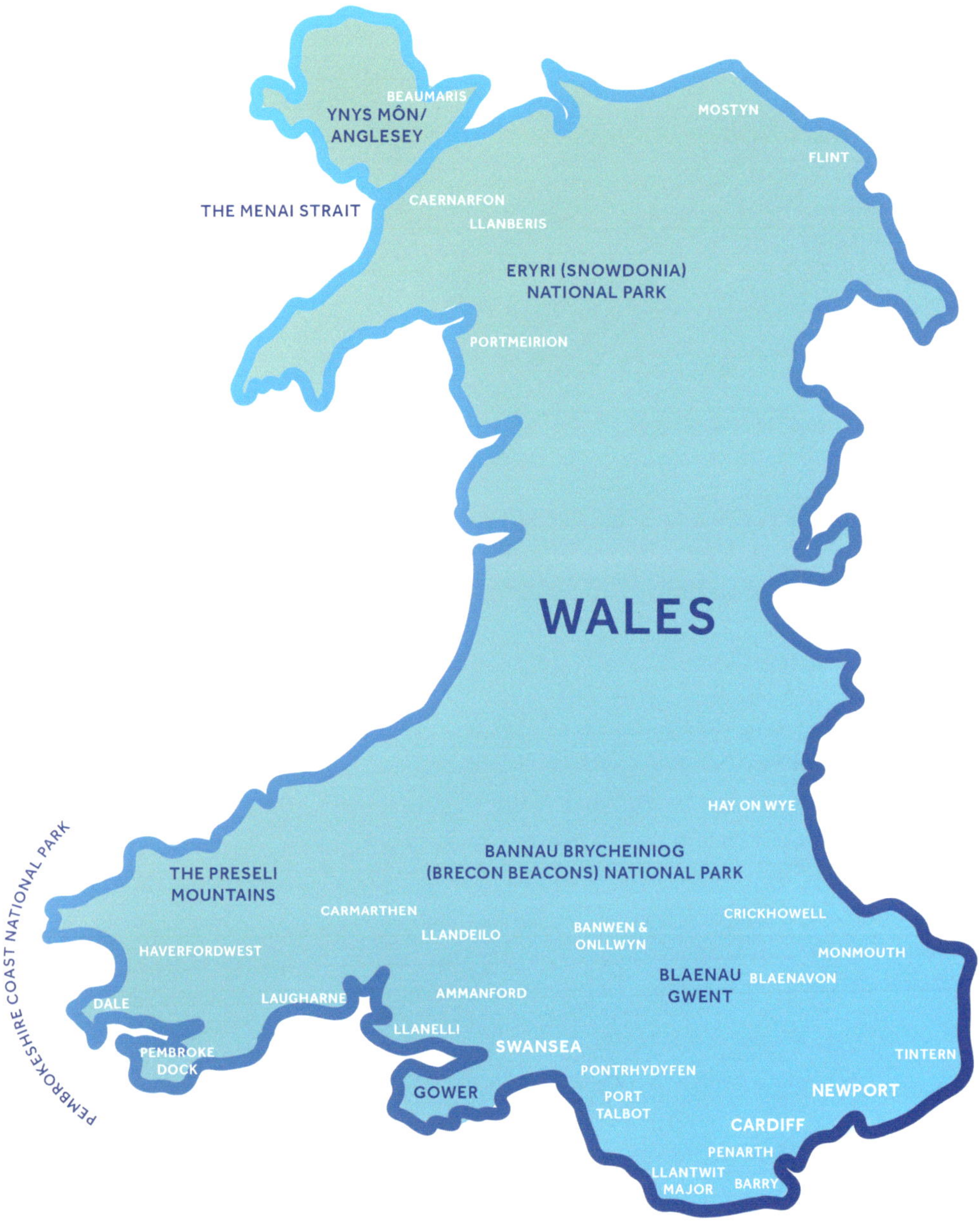
BEAUMARIS
YNYS MÔN/
ANGLESEY
MOSTYN
FLINT
THE MENAI STRAIT
CAERNARFON
LLANBERIS
ERYRI (SNOWDONIA)
NATIONAL PARK
PORTMEIRION
WALES
HAY ON WYE
PEMBROKESHIRE COAST NATIONAL PARK
BANNAU BRYCHEINIOG
(BRECON BEACONS) NATIONAL PARK
THE PRESELI
MOUNTAINS
CARMARTHEN
LLANDEILO
BANWEN &
ONLLWYN
CRICKHOWELL
HAVERFORDWEST
MONMOUTH
BLAENAU
GWENT
BLAENAVON
DALE
LAUGHARNE
AMMANFORD
LLANELLI
SWANSEA
PEMBROKE
DOCK
TINTERN
PONTRHYDYFEN
GOWER
PORT
TALBOT
NEWPORT
CARDIFF
PENARTH
LLANTWIT
MAJOR
BARRY

FOREWORD

by Celyn Jones

A Hollywood actor lived on the mountain in the town where I grew up throughout the 1980s. I never met him, never set eyes on him, but the idea of his presence alone was enough to set fire to my imagination. The town was Holyhead – or Caergybi – the island port town in north west Wales, and the actor was Gavan O'Herlihy, a familiar face on the big screen in the 70s and 80s as a henchman or soldier or cop or general baddie. He was in a Bond, and fought Charles Bronson in *Death Wish 3*, he even appeared in *Happy Days*. My Daidi chatted to him near the quarry a few times but that isn't the point. This isn't an unofficial biography of a much-loved cameo actor. This is an exploration of what happens when a drop of stardust contaminates the water we all drink… Suddenly, the world doesn't seem so big.

Let me paint you a picture that I'm sure many of you can relate to. This is working-class Britain, specifically Wales in my case. A time of four TV channels, of taping hits off the radio – there's one cinema in town for the few who can afford it and the holy grail is the VHS video shop... a portal of pure escapism, where the actors' names eclipse the titles of their films.

The world was not Hollywood, far from it, but Hollywood was in the ether and it always excited me. The potential and effect it could have on us if we got close to it, the extra to the ordinary… Has there ever been a better metaphor than the end of *The Wizard of Oz*, where Dorothy discovers that there is no grand wizard who will grant their wishes? It's just a sweaty guy behind a curtain making it all up…

Now that is showbusiness.

In *Adventures in the Screen Trade*, the late, great William Goldman said there is only one constant truth in the world of filmmaking, and that is: 'Nobody knows anything'. This can be frighteningly true but as I count myself amongst the dreamers and have always needed to have a little more hope to cling onto, I'd like to add to that by saying, '… until someone does something.'

This is a book with examples of people who *did* something; who made films, in Wales, for the world. We wanted to create an insightful and entertaining map and to pin to that map the stories of the extraordinary productions that have been made in our towns and under our skies. From wizards to werewolves, poets to kings, ravers to romantics, we have unearthed an embarrassment of riches and scratched the surface of a myriad of cinematic offerings.

As a nation, Wales has successfully exported teachers, writers, livestock, milk, music, coal, and now movies… So, maybe, in the future, children will say, 'I'm going to work down the studios like my mother and their father before them.'

"Filming *Six Minutes to Midnight* in Wales was a wonderful experience for me. As a kid whose first ever performance was at school in Swansea, it was amazing to be able to come back and perform in a film, shooting all over Wales. The people and the countryside were all very welcoming to us."

— SUZY EDDIE IZZARD

The seeds were sown in me a long time ago; seeds of wonder and never of doubt. I've been lucky to work as an actor in film and television for three decades and have written, directed and produced films for the past twelve years.

Every time my colleagues and I embark on a new project, I ask myself, 'What can be made in Wales? What if we brought this project to Wales?' I love that we, as a company, not only told these stories here, but in doing so we brought: Judi Dench to Llanelli where she discovered the delights of Joe's Ice Cream; Elijah Wood to Swansea, where he experienced Wind Street on a Friday night; Suzy Eddie Izzard to Llandudno where we transported the promenade and the locals to 1930's England; Rupert Everett to Caernarfon where he played Bingo on his nights off and Rebel Wilson to Wrexham, before Ryan Reynolds took over.

"[I] loved working in Wales and meeting the people who were always so kind and welcoming. And love that as part of my job I get to stay at places I never thought I'd usually travel to and experience the local delights!"
— REBEL WILSON, *The Almond and the Seahorse*

It's exciting to share these wondrous dreams with locals and to make them feel a part of it. There's the story of the film, and the story *in* the film – all of it contributing to our cultural experiences and landscape, and hopefully, moulding the next generations. As Orson Welles said, 'A writer needs a pen, an artist needs a brush, but a filmmaker needs an army.' Not wrong at all.

Films are mini-miracles and I applaud anyone who has made one, as it is virtually impossible to undertake the endeavour alone. The energy one needs to burn to get anything off the ground is enough to put off the hardiest of individuals. The drive, the ability to convince an army to join you

Below: Celyn on set for 'Madfabulous'

and build something – against all budgetary and scheduling odds – is remarkable and unusual.

Believe me when I say that the process is almost designed to break your heart at various points in its creation and evolution. From development to production, to post-production, to distribution and exhibition, including press and marketing, there are pitfalls at each turn and none of those chapters can guarantee a good film. Why would we do it, eh? Let's not think about that too much, as *this* book is not *that* book. This book is a celebration and not a health warning. It's a cheerleader for the brave armies who dreamed and willed their projects to life and did it on our doorsteps because they wanted to and they could.

However, for the sake of context and for those who need a little bit more information to appreciate what goes into it all or are just curious, please allow me to shed a little light on the process of bringing a film to life. So, here goes...

Firstly, it starts with a blank piece of paper and no money, and on that piece of paper goes an idea. The idea is then developed into a pitch or package, where the idea of the story is fleshed out into a concept – an example of what it might be and what it might look like. This would include the genre, budget, director, possible casting and other film comparisons, but there is still no money. The package might then get the attention of a production company or producer, who can further develop the idea and introduce it to a funding body or seed investor or other market partner. And maybe... *maybe*... they can find a little money for the writers to get a script written – but this is very risky money because it is very early in the process.

The script will then get written and that can take as long as it takes, with various drafts and notes. By now, the team is bigger with more people involved, investing their time, creativity and effort. So, now you have a script, and on one hand it's ready to be read by other creatives, like a director and actors (specifically, the lead actors – more on that in a minute). On the other hand, it needs to be costed up with a budget and schedule, so you know how much the actors, costumes, sets, music, crew, *etcetera*, will cost.

Every film is its own separate business and the budget has to cover everything from the cradle to the grave of the process; from that blank page to the delivery of the film. Value is the weight that hangs heavy around a filmmaker's neck, because nobody really knows anything and it isn't an exact science. The closest thing to de-risking a film is to have value in the package. And that value is in the genre, filmmakers and most likely in the lead actors – specifically, actors who are well-known and had previous success in similar genres – who are tried and tested so they come with a set value. For example, Will Ferrel in a comedy, Keanu Reeves in an action film, Meryl Streep in a drama, Denzel Washington in a prestige film and Tom Hanks in, well, anything. Horror is an interesting genre as it has a value of its own and doesn't require a famous face as the audience is loyal to it. Whereas drama is expensive to sell and market so it needs lots of well-known faces to have half a chance.

You now have a script, director, production company with producers, and a leading actor, all of which make the projected figures stack up. With these in place, it's time to get the money to make your film, so you go to the market. The market could be anything, from a studio who will pay you to make it, to a group of private investors who see a value and return or are keen to explore the business, to sales/finance markets at festivals, where an agent might pre-sell your film to various countries or territories upfront.

All the while, you are trying to reach that budget so you can make the film and get to work.

Think of film finance as a mortgage. To buy a house, you need a good credit history, a deposit and a secured salary with a set of accounts that can prove to a bank that you will return the mortgage plus interest, in exchange for owning a house. A film is not much different. You have your budget and it is made up of pre-sales, a small regional grant to stimulate the local economy, a little soft money from a film body who supports the industry, tax credit and maybe a gap financier, who believes in the future success of the made film, and can cover the investment against a few key territories. Eventually, the financial closing happens and you are now Green Lit.

Once you have the money, it has to be diligently spent to take the film through pre-production, where all the hiring is done, the locations are found and the building and making happens. Next comes the production stage, when the filming itself takes place, followed by post-production, where it is edited and all the sound is fixed and music added.

All in all, you've been at it for about a year by the time the film is delivered, not including the development period. From that point, you're exhausted, but now it's time to show it to the world, either straight to the audience via distribution or via a film festival launch to create buzz and interest. Quite often, especially in the independent film world, you have made a film without a buyer and you hope that the right person will be interested and take your baby into the world.

So, there you go... all that work with no guarantees and a great dollop of pressure and risk. It's not for the faint of heart but it is great when it works. Making a film with others is a collective experience and I always love the idea that the blank page becomes jobs, experiences and entertainment for many. It is magic and well worth the pain.

Above: Filming 'Madfabulous' on the Menai Strait

Ever since I started producing films myself, I grew an instant respect and empathy for others who do the same. When I act in films for others, I appreciate what it has taken to just get to that point of Green Light and, on set, I am a very sympathetic actor.

Back to our celebration of films made in Wales. The films in this book have all survived that process and not only lived to tell the tale but managed to etch their existence onto the cultural landscape: the mountain range of film and television. They have become quotes on t-shirts and funny memes that get shared, absorbed into our cultural identity and personality. They have launched careers and franchises, built businesses and filled art centres. Some are footnotes and others are corners of an anecdote but all of them are a story… A story pocketed by all who took part or witnessed the supernova of that planet colliding with that world, leaving its mark. It is no different from a cave drawing: history captured in a brief moment that has a chance of outlasting all involved.

Our nation is no longer a service industry for others to come and make their films in and leave, nor an anomaly like a humorous anecdote of when the circus once came to town. No, it has fast become a player, an incubator of talent and an industry of excellence. It isn't just for the castles and mountains they come now, but for the quality of craftsmanship and the can-do attitude of an army of storytellers.

"Without any exaggeration, the best crew I've ever worked with."

— DAME JUDI DENCH, on working in Wales for *Six Minutes to Midnight*

To dream up and make films in my own country is a privilege, an honour that I cherish.

When I started, it was audacious and too risky. 'No one makes films here!' – especially not me, with my background, and now it is as normal as bara brith and a part of our makeup. We don't have to leave to find a voice or stay to be heard. We can forge forward together because… why not? We also don't have to be invited or gain permission to make things happen. There are studios peppered up and down this small country with capacity to offer the most ambitious of canvases.

Arrogance? No, just progress. Everyone deserves the chance to work close to home. I had the opportunity to open a film studio, Aria Studios, on my home island of Anglesey and before the ribbon was cut, I remember saying, 'Ambition is critical, and if you build it they will come.' Neither quotes were my own but both appropriate, because come they have. Daniel Day Lewis, arguably one of the greatest living actors, decided to come out of retirement last year and he chose to shoot on Anglesey, because it not only offered privacy, expertise, a unique landscape but also offered the people and their mindset… people who made themselves available to the process. Now, isn't that just fantastic?

Each of the films highlighted in this book, and they are just the tip of the iceberg, were conjured up by people like us, for us. They rolled into the towns and contaminated the water with possibility, offering the everyday a chance to be on the silver screen, or to be as close to it as they wanted. Maybe they'd have a nugget of a story to keep forever of when that actor came to town, or the day they turned our street into that amazing thing, or covered our parks with a snow machine, or transported us back in time through the theatre of a period film.

For those moments, we all get to be Dorothy, to pull back that curtain and see what the magic really is. We all get to ride our metaphorical bikes through the Welsh streets to our imaginary video shop, with the knowledge that we too have a piece of Hollywood hiding up the mountain, keeping an eye on us, daring us to keep going.

A NOTE ON THE CONTENTS

by Frances Turpin

It's striking that many people in the film and television industry regard Wales as a unique place to film, from its spectrum of landscapes and lively towns to its vibrant capital and heritage coastlines. Couple geographical compactness with world-class production crews, and it's fair to say that Wales holds a special place in the hearts of many in the industry.

This book is not meant to be a comprehensive guide to every project ever filmed in Wales – such a collection would run to many more pages and take in many more films. Instead, it is a celebration of the way that Wales has captured the imagination of filmmakers, offering a glimpse from the other side of the camera, into the minds of those who have found Wales the perfect place to tell their stories.

It is worth noting that all of the projects in this book are in the English language. Wales is a bilingual country, and many excellent Cymraeg films and television shows have been, and continue to be, made here. We did not want to diminish the Welsh language film and TV industry by reducing their output to one or two inclusions in an already abbreviated collection.

The projects we've chosen to highlight are a mix of the new and the old; the cult classic and the soon-to-be favourite; the Hollywood blockbuster and the homegrown indie. They showcase the breadth of opportunity that Wales offers to location scouts, from the urban to the rural, the coastal sweep to the mountaintop, and everything in between. They show off the talent of the people who worked on them, too; the designers who turned 2010s Swansea into 1950s New York, the location managers who stood in quarries and saw alien planets, the directors who could see a story from a statistic, and the television producers who advocated for filming here.

You will find some familiar titles amongst these pages, but you may come across a few that you've never heard of before. We hope that, once you've finished reading, you'll track them down and watch them, before visiting some of these fantastic locations yourself to create your own stories in the landscapes that have been immortalised on film.

To put it more concisely:

"Wales has it all: the landscapes, the locations, the history, the ambition – but most of all it has the people. Some of the best crews, writers and producers in the world are based in Wales. We must work hard to ensure that remains the case."

— EDWARD THOMAS,
Location Manager for *Set Fire to the Stars, Doctor Who, Torchwood* and more

HOMEGROWN FILMS

**"It felt like I'd stepped into my own imagination.
It was like being a ghost inside my own head."**

—JOE DUNTHORNE, *WRITER OF SUBMARINE* (2010)

Yasmin Paige as Jordana in 'Submarine'

In this section, we explore a handful of 'home-grown' films – movies that were made in Wales in their entirety, or close enough to it.

Some, like *Pride* and *Madfabulous*, draw on real events from the nation's past, forever preserving stories that might otherwise be lost to time – such as the Lesbians and Gays Support the Miners alliance who helped to fund the miners' strike in a Valleys village, or the flamboyant Marquess who spent the majority of his family's millions on theatre and parties, and has since become a queer icon.

Many, indeed most, film Wales for Wales, give or take a few decades here and there. One – *Set Fire to the Stars* – transforms Wales into America. No matter where the story is set, it is clear that the Welsh settings have been inspirational and impact the films.

Overleaf: High Street, Cardiff, looking towards the castle

CAERDYDD
James Douglas

Human Traffic (1999)

DIRECTOR: JUSTIN KERRIGAN
WRITER: JUSTIN KERRIGAN
STARRING: JOHN SIMM, LORRAINE PILKINGTON, SHAUN PARKES, DANNY DYER
FILMED IN: CARDIFF, SOUTH WALES
LOCATIONS: GASSY JACKS PUB, SALISBURY ROAD; CLUB X, CHARLES STREET; PHILHARMONIC, ST. MARY'S STREET

ABOUT THE FILM

Once described as 'the last great film of the nineties' by *The Guardian*, *Human Traffic* combines 1990s rave culture with the concept of 'Cool Cymru.' The Welsh answer to 'Cool Britannia,' with bands like the Stereophonics, Manic Street Preachers, Catatonia and Super Furry Animals and films like *Twin Town* and *House of America*, Cool Cymru encapsulated a resurgence – or perhaps more accurately, a reshaping – of Welsh national pride and identity, all wrapped up in a very 90s aesthetic.

"To me, it's like a time capsule: it perfectly captures the end of the 90s. That's what it was like for millions of people every single weekend. It was a beautiful little snippet of time."

—JOHN SIMM,
speaking to *The Guardian* in 2022

Set in Cardiff, *Human Traffic* follows five friends in their early twenties who are living for the weekend, working (or not working, in the case of Danny Dyer's Moff) dead-end jobs Monday to Friday with the sole purpose of earning enough money and killing enough time to get to Friday night. The tagline of the film – 'the weekend is here' – encapsulates their common goal: go out, get high, have fun.

The action takes place over the course of one such Friday night as we follow Jip (John Simm), Lulu (Lorraine Pilkington), Koop (Shaun Parkes), Moff (Danny Dyer), Nina (Nicola Reynolds) and Nina's teenage brother Lee (Dean Davies) from pub to club to house party, to an inevitable Saturday morning comedown. Relationships are formed, threatened, and mended; alcohol is drunk; substances are taken; music is danced to; fun is had.

What singles *Human Traffic* out from other club culture films of the time is the lack of moralising – or demonising – around the actions of the characters; something that was important to Justin Kerrigan, the director and writer who was himself from Cardiff:

"I wanted to make a film about what me and my friends got up to on weekends… I purposely left out any scenes of dropping pills, and the film clearly discusses the paranoia and physiological effects of drugs. But, whatever the tabloid sensationalism at the time, I included no deaths as that was not my experience, nor that of anyone I knew."

—JUSTIN KERRIGAN,
speaking to *The Guardian* in 2022

Below: Westgate Street, Cardiff

Overleaf: The Prinicpality Stadium and surrounding areas

ABOUT THE LOCATION

While the majority of clubs and pubs that *Human Traffic* filmed in have since closed down and/or rebranded, fans of the film will still be able to find plenty of places to party in the same locations that the film used.

Westgate Street was used for external shots of the gang on their way to The Asylum club (in reality a combination of two clubs – Emporium on High Street, which closed in 2004, was used for external shots and Club X, an LGBTQ+ club on Charles Street which provided the dance floors, which closed in 2014). Today it sits in the shadow of the Principality Stadium (originally known as the Millennium Stadium), which opened the same year that *Human Traffic* premiered, and was still under construction during filming. The stadium is the home of Welsh rugby, as well as host to multiple major music events every year, including, in recent years, Beyoncé's Renaissance, and Taylor Swift's Eras Tour.

At the end of the film, Lulu and Jip walk arm in arm down the centre of St Mary Street – something possible in the film due to the late (or perhaps early, depending on perspective) hour. In 2010, the street was permanently pedestrianised as part of the development of the city's Castle Quarter, so lovebirds wanting to recreate this moment can do so at any time of day. No prizes for guessing which iconic Cardiff landmark overshadows this Quarter. While Cardiff Castle isn't actually shown in *Human Traffic*, the Norman motte and bailey castle, which sits in the centre of a courtyard built in the eighteenth century by the Bute family, is a must for any visitors to Cardiff.

Submarine (2010)

DIRECTOR: RICHARD AYOADE
WRITERS: RICHARD AYOADE, JOE DUNTHORNE
STARRING: CRAIG ROBERTS, YASMIN PAIGE, SALLY HAWKINS, NOAH TAYLOR, PADDY CONSIDINE
FILMED IN: SOUTH WALES
LOCATIONS: SWANSEA, BARRY, PONTSTICILL RESERVOIR (BANNAU BRYCHEINIOG/ BRECON BEACONS), PAGET ROOMS (PENARTH), BISHOP GORE SCHOOL (SWANSEA),

ABOUT THE FILM

Written, filmed, and set in south Wales, *Submarine* is a quintessential 'homegrown' film. Based on the 2008 novel of the same name by Welsh writer Joe Dunthorne and set in 1980s Swansea, the film follows socially awkward teenager Oliver (Craig Roberts) as he navigates the twin goals of losing his virginity by his sixteenth birthday and preventing his mum (Sally Hawkins) from leaving his dad (Noah Taylor).

Oppostie: Craig Roberts as Oliver

Below: A birdseye view of Barry

ABOUT THE LOCATION

While a handful of south Wales towns and areas were used as settings for *Submarine*, it is Swansea – Oliver's hometown – that most influences the plot and overall aesthetic of the film. Sitting on the coast and with the river Tawe running through it (the Cymraeg name is 'Abertawe' which translates to 'mouth of the Tawe'), Swansea was known as 'Copperopolis' during the Industrial Revolution, and along with neighbouring Port Talbot and Cardiff, was a hive of industry during its peak.

For Dunthorne, who grew up in Swansea, and drew on his own memories when writing the novel, there was never any doubt about the location for the cinematic adaptation; although Sheffield, where the film's production company Warp Films is based – and which shares an industrial (and specifically metalworking) history with Swansea – was briefly considered.

"The book is intimately tied to Swansea and Gower, right down to the chapter headings. For me it felt as though Oliver's personality was connected to that contradictory view from his window in Swansea, the steelworks in one direction and the beaches in the other, industry and nature glaring at each across the bay. I also felt that the very particular culture of south Wales – both very Welsh and yet somehow not Welsh enough – hadn't often been seen on screen and I wanted to change that."

Below: The Swansea skyline

Opposite: The Pontsticill Reservoir

The shots of the film reflect this dichotomy between the urban/industrial and the rural. Oliver especially, despite living in a built-up area, is often seen in fairly remote, abandoned-looking places which hint at the area's history, such as the overgrown railway bridge columns and an abandoned bathtub.

"I vividly remember arriving on set to watch some of the school scenes. The set designers had put a new sign above the school gates so that it had the same name from the book. They'd even made a school uniform for this fictional school. At first, I couldn't see the cameras, just the actors running around in the playground, performing a scene from the book – and it felt like I'd stepped into my own imagination. It was like being a ghost inside my own head."

— JOE DUNTHORNE,
Writer

Below: Oliver in the abandoned bathtub on the outskirts of Swansea

Opposite top: Paddy Considine as Graham and Sally Hawkins as Jill in Swansea

Opposite bottom: Craig Roberts as Oliver

OPEN
THE PASSION OF JOAN OF ARC
An Immortal Screen Classic that will live Forever!
WITH
FALCONETTI
The World's Most Outstanding
ENGLISH DIALOGUE
BY

Pride (2014)

DIRECTOR: MATTHEW WARCHUS
WRITER: STEPHEN BERESFORD
STARRING: BILL NIGHY, IMELDA STAUNTON, DOMINIC WEST, ANDREW SCOTT
FILMED IN: SOUTH WALES
LOCATIONS: LLANDEILO, BANWEN, ONLLWYN, CASTELL CARREG CENNEN

Based on real-life events, *Pride* tells the story of a group of queer activists – known as 'Lesbians and Gays Support the Miners' – who, in the midst of the 1984 Miners' Strike, travel to a Welsh village in the Dulais Valley in order to bring money they have raised in support of the miners' families directly to them. After some initial misgivings and prejudice, the two communities soon bond over their shared experiences of oppression and marginalisation by Thatcher's government.

"The film is about 70% true and 30% invention – but Stephen Beresford is spot on showing how warm the welcome was from almost everyone."

—JONATHAN BLAKE,
played by Dominic West in *Pride*,
to the BBC in 2015

Photographs: Behind-the-scenes photos of 'Pride' filming in Banwen, courtesy of Penny Skuse

ABOUT THE LOCATION

The 1984 Miners' Strike lasted a year, affecting communities – primarily in Wales, Scotland and northern England – across the UK. The strike, in response to the planned mass closure of pits in England, was ultimately unsuccessful, acting as a rapid catalyst for the dismantling of the British coal industry and its 187,000-strong workforce. This led to a period of intense financial struggle for former miners and their families.

The south Wales valleys, including Dulais, were one of the areas that grew exponentially during the industrial revolution, with coal mining being the foundation that most communities were built on. Onllwyn, where the real events took place, was the first industrial village in the Dulais Valley. Filming for *Pride* took place in Onllwyn as well as several towns nearby, including Banwen, where visitors can see a memorial stone for St Patrick, the patron saint of Ireland, who is believed to have been born in the area before being taken to Ireland at the age of sixteen.

The disco scenes, in which the two groups bond over disco music (specifically the song 'Shame, Shame, Shame' by Shirley & Company) was filmed at the Onllwyn Miners Welfare Hall – where the original Lesbian and Gays Support the Miners' Group arrived with their donation. As the name suggests, the Hall was opened with the aim of supporting local mining families, providing a place for the community to gather, watch films, and play sports. In 2015 the Hall hosted a reunion between the two groups to mark the thirtieth anniversary of their connection.

Some filming also took place at Castell Carreg Cennen, in Carmarthenshire, which was once voted the 'most romantic ruin in Wales' by *Countryfile* magazine. The remains of Castell Carreg Cennen can be dated back to the thirteenth century, but there is evidence that the site – strategically located at the top of a hill – had been occupied long before, as both Roman coins and prehistoric skeletons have been found by archaeologists. The castle also features a natural limestone cave, which visitors who don't mind the dark can explore.

Below: Houses in Llandeilo

Opposite: Castell Carreg Cennen by Ken Day

Set Fire to the Stars (2014)

DIRECTOR: ANDY GODDARD
WRITERS: ANDY GODDARD, CELYN JONES
STARRING: ELIJAH WOOD, CELYN JONES, KELLY REILLY
FILMED IN: SOUTH WALES
LOCATIONS: SWANSEA

ABOUT THE FILM

Unusual on this list of homegrown films, *Set Fire to the Stars* was filmed, but not set, in Wales. Instead, the streets of Swansea were transformed using black and white filming and clever set dressing into 1950s New York, where aspiring poet John Malcolm Brinnin (Elijah Wood) invites the legendary Welsh poet Dylan Thomas (Celyn Jones). The semi-biographical story is scored by original music by Gruff Rhys of Welsh band Super Furry Animals, proving that a story does not need to be set in Wales to be intrinsically Welsh.

"Dylan Thomas was everything. Poet, rockstar, icon. He blazed a trail and his personality and talent burnt into my mind. There aren't any moving images of him, any colour pictures or voice recordings of his non-performative voice, so he exists in our imaginations and hearts. It made sense to film in black and white and play him with all the contrasts and colours of humanity I could conjure; he was everything to many, so everyone he had to be. Being directed by Andy Goddard, acting opposite Elijah Wood to a Gruff Rhys score was an embarrassment of riches. Making *Set Fire to the Stars* the way we did, writing it the way we did and playing him was one of the greatest pleasures of my career and life."

— CELYN JONES,
Writer and Actor

Previous spread: Celyn Jones as Dylan Thomas in 'Set Fire to the Stars'

Opposite: Elijah Wood as John M. Brinnin

Overleaf: Celyn and Elijah Wood on set in Swansea

SBM 143

Below: Swansea skyline

ABOUT THE LOCATION

Dylan Thomas, author of *Under Milk Wood*, is Swansea's most famous son – he was said to have been inspired greatly by his hometown, and poet and city are intrinsically linked. His birthplace and childhood home, 5 Cwmdonkin Drive, is now a living museum dedicated to the poet. The Dylan Thomas Centre is also located in Swansea, and the Dylan Thomas Prize – one of the most prestigious in literature – is hosted by Swansea University. The local theatre is named after him.

Perhaps it is the deep connection between Swansea and Dylan that caused *Set Fire to the Star*'s production designer Edward Thomas (described by the location manager Gareth Skelding as 'a Swansea boy who wants to make Swansea look incredible'), to have this reaction to the suggestion of the film being made elsewhere:

"When I was first asked to be involved in the film it was suggested to me that we shoot it in Manchester. As a lifelong Dylan Thomas and Vernon Watkins fan I simply answered, "Not on my watch". If we are making a movie about Dylan Thomas, then it needs to be shot in Swansea.

"Swansea provided the perfect architecture for the movie, from the street scenes on Adelaide Street to the interiors of the Brangwyn and the No Sign Wine Bar in Wind Street offering us our version of the White Horse Tavern, a regular watering hole frequented by Dylan in New York."

— EDWARD THOMAS,
Production Designer

"Doing [*Set Fire to the Stars*] was a completely different spin, and put a different light on what we shot – Swansea for New York, in black and white, at Christmas, with Elijah Wood… Some of the visuals are fantastic, and I think the decision to shoot that in black and white really made that… That's a film that didn't have that much money, you know, we were trying to think outside the box."

— GARETH SKELDING,
Location Manager

The film was shot in black and white to evoke 1950s New York

The Toll (2021)

RELEASED IN THE US AS *THE TOLLBOOTH.*
DIRECTOR: RYAN ANDREW HOOPER
WRITER: MATT REDD
STARRING: MICHAEL SMILEY, ANNES ELWY, IWAN RHEON
FILMED IN: PEMBROKESHIRE
LOCATIONS: ROYAL NAVAL AIR STATION, DALE (HAVERFORDWEST), CLEDDAU BRIDGE, NOLTON HAVEN (HAVERFORDWEST), PEMBROKE DOCK, THE PRESELI MOUNTAINS

ABOUT THE FILM

In *The Toll*, a comedic Welsh Western, Michael Smiley plays an unnamed man known to locals only as Toll Booth, on account of his job on a rural Welsh toll road. However, our protagonist is a not-quite-former criminal, hiding from his past in the one place nobody would ever think to look. His new enterprise collides with a chance encounter from his previous life, while local police officer Catrin (Annes Elwy), who until now has been more used to dealing with parking tickets and fly tipping than organised crime, begins to circle.

Below: The storage container, filmed at the Royal Naval Air Station, Dale

Opposite Top: Michael Smiley, Iwan Rheon, Paul Kaye and Gary Beadle in 'The Toll' (Signature Entertainment)

Opposite bottom: Annes Elwy in 'The Toll' (Signature Entertainment)

Previous spread: Nolton Haven, where Catrin tries to track down her surfing colleagues

ABOUT THE LOCATION

Pembrokeshire is the UK's only coastal national park and has multiple areas of Outstanding Natural Beauty. A number of its beaches will crop up later in this book; several in blockbuster fantasy films.

It is also an area with a sparse population in ratio to land, with miles of untouched coastline as well as an agricultural past and present leading to large areas of crop and grazing land. Pembroke Dock, which is featured in *The Toll*'s opening scenes, is one of the larger towns in the area, and is home to the Cleddau Bridge (across which an ambulance drives in an aerial shot in the film). Suitably, in 2019, this became the last bridge in Wales to close its toll booths and become free to pass over.

The Preseli mountains are wild and ancient. Bronze Age burial cairns and Iron Age forts are scattered between craggy rocks and stretches of moorland. On a clear day, both Ireland and Eryri (Snowdonia) in north Wales, can be seen across the sea.

"Pembrokeshire drove the narrative of the story. I can't remember if it was [writer Matt Redd] or I, but one of us read that Pembrokeshire had the lowest crime rate in the country. I liked the idea that rather than the reason being [that] there just wasn't that much crime, it was actually due to the fact that the criminals were really good at not being caught. My reflections on the place as a visitor worked alongside Matt's understanding of the area as a local. I think we both felt it was a bit wild as an area and that inspired the idea of *The Toll* as a 'West-Walian Western'."

— RYAN ANDREW HOOPER,
Director

Below: A behind-the-scenes shot of the Preseli Mountains

Opposite: The Cleddau Bridge

"Matt and I were determined that *The Toll* would celebrate Wales as we experienced and understood it. Wales is often presented on screen as a slightly daft or dopey place; it's a stereotype I don't recognise nor would want to lionise on screen. I think Wales, and Pembrokeshire in particular, is weird. It's a strange mishmash of things, ancient and anachronistic at times. It's incredibly tribal, each village has its own identity that's often defined by its opposition to the next village over. It's sceptical and welcoming at the same time. That dichotomy of place is embedded in the story – Tollbooth Man is both the most pointless and the most important person in the area. I don't think this is unique to Wales as a concept but the specific realities of it are. This story would not have worked anywhere else; there would have been different elements to be incorporated.

"The Preseli mountains were amazing, they're so epic and the final shot [of the film] came about when I looked through the viewfinder as the DP was zooming out and understood the sheer scale of the place. The booth itself was great but had its own challenges – we were literally on the edge of a cliff in December and got the full force of the weather rolling in off the Atlantic. We bought a booth and fitted it out, it became Michael's little safe haven, a place he grew attached to as it was so much part of his character. Wales' location options are incredible; we found everything we needed in a pretty small radius.

"I think maybe my favourite moment was during the shootout. It was a night shoot, and we had most of the actors there. The wind and rain [were] howling and we were hoping for a break in the weather to film. The actors and I all piled into a small trailer, stuffed in like sardines and we started working on the script as it felt like there was too much dialogue. I had the opportunity to pause and realise what was going on – there were a bunch of people, in a tiny caravan, on a cliff top in west Wales all immersed in the characters to the point they knew them better than anyone. It sort of encapsulated what film-making is – a ragtag bunch of people playing make-believe, having fun and being silly. It's an astonishing amount of effort to go through just to get back to doing what every 8-year-old does on a daily basis."

— RYAN ANDREW HOOPER,
Director

With breathtaking shots of mountainsides cutting to a father and son playing cards in a pub, and an Englishman mistaking locals speaking Welsh for a 'foreign' language, *The Toll* is a film that feels Welsh from head to toe – with just a little bit more violence thrown in, for drama.

(Both photographs in this spread) – Behind-the-scenes pictures from filming at the Royal Navy Air Station, courtesy of Ryan Andrew Hooper.

Opposite: Samantha Morton as Liz Evans in 'Save the Cinema' (Future Artists Entertainment)

Save the Cinema (2022)

DIRECTOR: SARA SUGARMAN
WRITERS: SCREENPLAY BY PIERS ASHWORTH, BASED ON STORY BY LORRAINE KING
STARRING: SAMANTHA MORTON, JONATHAN PRYCE, TOM FELTON
FILMED IN: CARMARTHENSHIRE, WEST WALES
LOCATIONS: CARMARTHEN (KING STREET AND THE LYRIC THEATRE), AMMANFORD TOWN HALL, LAUGHARNE AND LLANDEILO

ABOUT THE FILM

Set in the 1990s, *Save the Cinema* re-tells the real-life story of Liz Evans (Samantha Morton), a hairdresser and local theatre manager from Carmarthen. With the help of fellow local film-lovers, Liz hatches a plan to save the local cinema by convincing Stephen Spielberg (yes, that one) to release *Jurassic Park* at their local Lyric Theatre on the same night as its UK premiere.

"I am always drawn to strong Welsh women whose life is based on love and service. So it was a no-brainer to read [Liz's] story and how she saved a cinema in order to nourish children with an education to set them up for life. In the Welsh way! With Welsh values! I have no choice [but to make films in Wales]. My soul sings only when I tell a Welsh story. Hiraeth is in my heart and soul."

— SARA SUGARMAN,
Director

Below: Behind-the-scenes of filming in the Lyric Theatre, courtesy of Sara Sugarman.

Overleaf: Tom Felton as Richard Goodridge (Future Artists Entertainment)

ABOUT THE LOCATION

Filmmakers were able to recreate the events of the time by filming at the Lyric on King Street in Carmarthen. Much of the rest of the action was filmed nearby, close to where the real-life characters lived and worked. Originally built in 1854 and updated with the current stage and auditorium in 1936, the Lyric is the largest theatre in the county of Carmarthenshire and is operational to this day, with regular screenings and productions. According to some, the ghost of Liz Evans (affectionately known as 'Liz the Lyric') has been spotted from time to time

"Filming in the Lyric Theatre was a rare and meaningful opportunity, only possible due to the unusual circumstances of the Covid lockdown. As Production Designer for *Save the Cinema*, it was a privilege to help transform the space into a version of its former self. What made the experience especially memorable was working alongside local people who had lived through the very period we were depicting. Their insight, generosity, and care for the story brought a quiet authenticity to everything we created."

—JONATHAN HOULDING,
Production Designer

"I love when I can ground [a film] in reality, and being with those who loved Liz and carry on where she left off in this wonderful town in this wonderful theatre full of her spirit – and may I add, her wonderful sons – made me proud to tell her story.

"It was lockdown, so only twenty extras were allowed – and yet the script said, 'three hundred people watch *How Green Was My Valley*.' So we got mannequins in, and I gave the mannequins acting notes by mistake!"

— SARA SUGARMAN,
Director

Opposite: Filming at the Lyric Theatre, courtesy of Sara Sugarman

Below: The entrance to the Lyric, taken back into the 90s by the filmmakers (Future Artists Entertainment)

Chuck Chuck Baby (2023)

DIRECTOR: JANIS PUGH
WRITER: JANIS PUGH
STARRING: LOUISE BREALEY, ANNABEL SCHOLEY, CELYN JONES
FILMED IN: NORTH WALES
LOCATIONS: FLINT, MOSTYN, AND SURROUNDING AREAS

ABOUT THE FILM

Chuck Chuck Baby is a musical drama set in a chicken factory, which explores finding yourself, and queer love, later in life.

Helen (Louise Brealey) is stuck in a life she no longer wants (and perhaps never did), working nights processing chicken and living with her ex-husband, his new girlfriend, their new baby and her dying mother-in-law (Sorcha Cusack) – the only person she still feels loves her. Cue the return of Helen's childhood crush Joanne (Annabel Scholey), who 'got out' of their hometown, but is back to confront her demons. Romance and musical numbers blossom as, surrounded by chicken factory friends and colleagues, the two reconnect.

The film was written and directed by Janis Pugh, and is influenced heavily by her own early life in north Wales:

"I write from the heart, so I write stories that are personal to me.

"I was brought up in Flint, north Wales, surrounded by strong, dynamic working-class women; their tangible force of energy is something I have always tried to reflect in my work. Their resilience, strength, and humour are very much shaped by the landscape of Flintshire, which itself is an important character in the film. Rural meets industrial, which creates a rugged steeliness to the characters that I personally feel is unique to that area and very much connected to my soul as a filmmaker. I couldn't think of shooting that film anywhere else.

"All the locations in the film were part of my childhood playing ground. The blue bridge holds many memories for me, and I absolutely love it, which surprises a lot of my friends from home."

—JANIS PUGH,
Director

Opposite: The lighthouse on Talacre beach, where some scenes were filmed

Overleaf: Helen and Joanne visit the TSS Duke of Lancaster (Artemesia Films)

ABOUT THE LOCATION

Located close to the English border in north Wales, Flint is a coastal town most famous for Flint Castle, one of Edward I's strongholds during his invasion of Wales. Nearby is the Flint Marsh, now popular with bird watchers, and the Dee Estuary. As the film reveals, the area has an industrial past and present which has shaped the community as well as the landscape, most notably with the beached forward passenger ship the TSS *Duke of Lancaster*, which has been grounded at Llannerch-y-Mor Wharf since 1979.

Janis explains that being able to use the ship as a location for filming was a highlight of the shoot for her, as was being able to invite some of her former colleagues to participate in the film:

"I think the *Duke of Lancaster* ship, which has been sitting on the north Wales coast for many years, was [particularly] special. When I was growing up it was a market and fun ship which was a great day out for us kids. It is a big, beautiful, rusted metaphor that speaks volumes about lost industries and left-behind towns. It was about placing the characters near it and letting the ship tell the rest of the story.

"There are so many [memories from filming]. But the stand-out must be working with the original chicken factory women for the factory scenes. At the end of the film, we show intimate portraits of the women in the factory. Those women are the women I worked with at the chicken factory when I was sixteen. They brought chicken packing knowledge, humour and amazing energy to the set. It really was very special, and I truly believe it wouldn't have been the same without them."

—JANIS PUGH,
Director

Opposite top: The chicken factory girls run across Janis' favourite blue bridge (Artemesia Films)

Opposite bottom: Courtesy of Artemesia Films

Madfabulous (2025)

DIRECTOR: CELYN JONES
WRITER: LISA BAKER
STARRING: RUPERT EVERETT, CALLUM SCOTT HOWELLS, LOUISE BREALEY
FILMED IN: NORTH WALES
LOCATIONS: PLAS NEWYDD, YNYS MÔN/ANGLESEY, GLYNLLIFON (CAERNARFON)

ABOUT THE FILM

Madfabulous tells the story of Henry Cyril Paget, the Fifth Marquess of Anglesey, who famously spent almost all of his family's vast fortune on theatre, parties, and an extravagant lifestyle, before dying in near poverty at only twenty-nine. Scandalous at the time and later almost erased from history by his own family, Paget defied societal expectations of class and gender. The film, shot at the Paget's ancestral home, Plas Newydd, is as loud, colourful and glamorous as its subject.

"When the sun comes out, you go for amazing walks. There are a lot of nice pubs in Caernarfon. It's an amazing town."

— RUPERT EVERETT,
Actor

Below: Siobhán McSweeney as Blanche and Callum Scott Howells as Henry Paget (Mad as Birds)

Opposite: Sailing on the Menai Strait (Mad as Birds)

"It was a privilege to shine a cultural light on my homeland, because I grew up never seeing the place where I lived represented on screen. But our quiet backwater had been home to the most extraordinary character I could ever have imagined, whose madcap pursuits had been reported internationally, due to his exceptional talent for self-promotion. There was no better place to make the film but on Anglesey and with local talent who felt just as I did about these precious islands, which were once the seat of Henry Paget, dressed as a queen in ropes of pearls and glittering diamonds and living by standards which are utterly current today."

— LISA BAKER,
Writer

Below: Filmed at Glynllifon

ABOUT THE LOCATION

Over 550 years old, Plas Newydd (meaning 'new hall') is located on the island of Anglesey or Ynys Môn in north Wales. A beautiful, ivy-covered house, it has been home to the Paget family since the 1780s. Despite being primarily a National Trust property since 1976, the Pagets still keep a residential suite at the home. Visitors can tour the lower floors and view a 17.5 metre-long, floor-to-ceiling mural painted by Rex Whistler, full of references to family history in what was once a dining room. Those inclined to do so can also view the wooden leg of the First Marquess of Anglesey, which he required after losing his own in the Battle of Waterloo. The house overlooks the Menai Strait and is surrounded by Grade 1 listed landscaping, including two Neolithic burial mounds.

"It is my *Madfabulous* summer and I'm driving over the Britannia Bridge from mainland Wales to Anglesey. I look left, as I always do, to catch a glimpse of the Nelson monument, Kyffin Williams' house, and just further down the straits I see Plas Newydd, the home of the Marquess of Anglesey and our location for the week.

"As a local lad, coming home to shoot and direct this film is a big plus and to play with the big posh house is definitely one for the memories. We had just spent a month filming our interiors at a disused manor house, Glynllifon, in Caernarfon, and now it's time to grab our majestic exteriors. The weather gods are smiling on us, thank goodness, because we have no option than to get it all this week before cast and budget disappear.

"Filming in a protected National Trust property is a tough beast to navigate, not only with the visitors and opening times but also for the fact that everything inside is protected. So lights, furniture and movement become very slow and delicate and not very flexible – also, very expensive. Hence, we shoot the interiors elsewhere where we have more control and flexibility. Today we have a sailboat, all principal cast, horse & cart and the most ambitious part of the film… the ending.

"We capture the farewells, the chases and the stunts. We chew up and use every corner available to us to fill our story and give us scale. The second camera is capturing the building, surrounding areas and changing light that will help the edit and film to breathe. We have one more hour to film the arrival of Henry on the boat and for that we need to board the vessel with the crew and cast, sail up the Menai Straits and return as we film the approach.

"That short sailing trip forces us to look, reflect and share the moment… We look back at the house from the water, take in the set decorations on the lawn, the immaculately dressed cast and the people ready to receive us. Look at what we are doing, what we've done and with who... All this effort and creativity towards a common, shared goal… My heart swells with pride: it's a good day in the office."

— CELYN JONES,
Director

Overleaf: Plas Newydd

Mr Burton (2025)

DIRECTOR: MARC EVANS
WRITERS: TOM BULLOUGH, JOSH HYAMS
STARRING: TOBY JONES, HARRY LAWTEY, LESLEY MANVILLE
FILMED IN: SOUTH WALES
LOCATIONS: PORT TALBOT, AFAN VALLEY, PONTRHYDYFEN, MARGAM CASTLE

ABOUT THE FILM

Another recent addition, and another film about an iconic Welsh figure, *Mr Burton* tells the story of how Richard Jenkins (Harry Lawtey), son of a miner, became Richard Burton, internationally famous film star and accomplished stage actor, under the tutelage of his teacher Philip Burton (Toby Jones). It was Philip who saw the potential in Richard, helping him to get his first acting job and encouraging him into further education.

With the blessing of his birth father, Richard became Philip's legal ward, taking his surname as an homage. The film takes a look at Richard's early days as an actor, as he thrives under Philip's training and has to learn to face the prejudice held against his working-class background by the industry he wants to break into.

ABOUT THE LOCATION

Richard Burton was born in Pontrhydyfen in the Afan Valley in 1925, and grew up in Taibach, Port Talbot. While he moved away to pursue fame in Hollywood, his family stayed in the area, and he was known to visit throughout his life, sometimes bringing along Elizabeth Taylor, whom he famously married twice (once in 1964 until 1974, then again in 1975 until 1976).

There is a renowned photograph of Richard Burton and his father Dic Jenkins on the Pontrhydyfen Aqueduct, a local landmark which was built between 1824 and 1827 to fuel the waterwheels at a nearby Ironworks. The bridge was restored in 2017 and it is still visited often by fans wishing to recreate the scene.

Similar to nearby Swansea and Cardiff, Port Talbot's history was shaped significantly by the Industrial Revolution, leading it to become home to the largest steelworks in the United Kingdom.

Opposite: Toby Jones as Philip Burton, Harry Lawtey as Richard Burton taken on Pontrhydyfen Viaduct. Photo by Warren Orchard ©Severn Burton Ltd

Overleaf: Harry Lawtey as Richard Burton, taken on Mynydd Margam. Photo by Warren Orchard ©Severn Burton Ltd

KING HENRY V.
A. W. VERITY

"Shooting in Wales for me is often a conversation with the past, remembered or imagined. Often we are searching for something that we know may not exist. Yet I am always surprised when we find what we're looking for around corners, tucked away and untouched. With *Mr Burton* we were trying to capture a world that has almost completely disappeared (industrial wartime south Wales) and found vestiges of it across the Valleys, allowing us to build our film. When we walked the actors across the aqueduct in Pontrhydyfen... there was a thrilling sense of cultural déjà vu, of memories and dreams melding. Beyond the buildings and the towns there is the landscape of course, this glorious hinterland with its western light, between mountain and sea. These natural elements are always characters in our stories: tough, gnarly and enduring. Admittedly, they can be a bit moody at times but they are always there for us and always inspire."

— MARC EVANS,
Director

Below: Pontrhydyfen Viaduct

Opposite: (Both images) Memorials to Richard Burton in his hometown

Richard Burton
"GNASHER"
'there is one place you belong to, and in my case it's Pontrhydyfen'
GŴYL BONT BURTON
BURTON BONT FESTIVAL

Croeso Welcome
MAN GENI
BIRTHPLACE OF
RICHARD BURTON
IVOR EMMANUEL
REBECCA EVANS
PONTRHYDYFEN

HOLLYWOOD COMES TO VISIT

"From its vast beauty across both sea and sand dunes to its unique, west-facing position, we knew this location would provide the creative and cinematic qualities the much-loved book adaptations deserved."

— SUE QUINN, LOCATION MANAGER FOR *HARRY POTTER AND THE DEATHLY HALLOWS.*

'Shell Cottage' on Freshwater West, by Illtud Llyr Dunsford

Imagine bumping into Thor dressed as a fairy-tale knight on your daily dog walk, spotting the hero of Gotham on your way to the shops, or discovering a shrine to a house-elf as you search for the perfect picnic spot.

While Wales may have produced some of Hollywood's biggest names in the last century, it is not a one-way exchange. From standing in for the Yorkshire moors in an iconic 80s horror-comedy and providing the backdrop to multiple epic fantasy films to hiding the Bat Cave, Hollywood has leant on Wales numerous times throughout the years when it comes to locations for a scene or two.

In this section we look at some of the bigger budget films that have paid a visit to different parts of Wales. We look at why they were chosen, and how they were dressed up to play the part.

An American Werewolf in London (1981)

DIRECTOR: JOHN LANDIS
WRITER: JOHN LANDIS
STARRING: GRIFFIN DUNNE, DAVID NAUGHTON
FILMED IN: BANNAU BRYCHEINIOG AND THE BLACK MOUNTAINS
LOCATIONS: CRICKADARN, HAY BLUFF

ABOUT THE FILM

A cult classic comic-horror film from the 1980s, *An American Werewolf in London* does more or less what it says on the tin. Recent American graduates Davis Kessler (David Naughton) and Jack Goodman (Griffin Dunne) take a trip across the pond and, while hiking across the North York Moors, find themselves in a familiar scene to any fan of monster horrors. Having a drink in a pub, the broad-accented, chess-playing locals fall suddenly silent upon being asked about an occult-looking star on the wall, and advise the pair to, "Stay on the road, keep clear of the moors," and "Beware the moon, lads."

Of course, it wouldn't be a horror film without the protagonists ignoring this advice, and later that night they are attacked, with David waking up several weeks later in a hospital in London. The name of the film should give you a pretty good clue as to what happens next…

"We filmed the moors scenes in Wales… there was this moment when [Griffin Dunne and David Naughton] were out walking – it was freezing and Griffin's nose started running. He thought I'd called "Cut" but I hadn't, so by the end of the sequence he was just wiping his nose and almost giggling. We left it in: it gave the scenes a wonderfully real feeling."

—JOHN LANDIS,
Director, speaking to *The Guardian* in 2017

ABOUT THE LOCATION

Despite having America and London in its title, the film actually uses places in Bannau Brycheiniog (the Brecon Beacons) to stand in for the Yorkshire Moors and the small village of Crickadarn was used as the fictional 'East Proctor', which the hapless protagonists stumble across. The opening shots of the moors were filmed on the Hay Bluff in Powys, not far from the famous book town of Hay-on-Wye. The Bluff is a great place to walk or cycle – so long as you stay on the road and beware the moon!

Previous spread and below: Hay Bluff, where Davis and Jack go on their ill-advised hike...

Willow (1988)

DIRECTOR: RON HOWARD
WRITER: BOB DOLLMAN
STARRING: WARWICK DAVIS, VAL KILMER, JOANNE WHALLEY
FILMED IN: NORTH WALES, ERYRI (SNOWDONIA) NATIONAL PARK
LOCATION: DINORWIG QUARRY, NORTH WALES, LLANBERIS, GWYNEDD

ABOUT THE FILM

Willow (Warwick Davis), a farmer and aspiring sorcerer, undertakes a journey across a fantasy land in order to reunite a baby girl with her people. Seemingly abandoned in a river near his home, Willow discovers that her mother had sent her away deliberately, in the hope of keeping her safe. Born with a distinctive birthmark that has revealed her as the subject of a prophecy, her birth signals the downfall of the evil queen Bavmorda (Jean Marsh). Willow is joined on his adventure by, amongst others, his friend Meegosh (David Steinberg) and a swordsman named Madmartigan (Val Kilmer).

A sequel series to the film was released in 2022. Also filmed in Wales, locations included Morlais Park, Eryri (Snowdonia) National Park, Merthyr Mawr, Pendine Sands, Neath Abbey, and Taf Fechan Forest. The series picks up twenty years after the end of the film, with Willow (reprised by Warwick Davis) facing new challenges when the Prince, Airk (Dempsey Bryk), is kidnapped and his sister Kit (Ruby Cruz) assembles a group of unlikely heroes to rescue him.

"Creative Wales/Welsh Government has enjoyed a long-standing relationship with Lynwen Brennan CBE (President and General Manager of Lucasfilm), who hails from Tenby. In 2018 we hosted her and her Disney colleagues for a studio recce, and the following year we were invited to explore potential stage space and filming locations for *Willow*. With iconic sequences from the original 1988 film shot in north Wales, it was only fitting that the story should return – once again positioning Wales on the global stage."

— PENNY SKUSE,
Wales Screen Commission

Opposite: Piles of slate at Dinorwig Quarry

Overleaf: Dinorwig Quarry, looking down towards Llyn Peris

ABOUT THE LOCATION

An active slate mine from 1787 to 1969, Dinorwig Quarry is now part of a UNESCO World Heritage Site, the 'Slate Landscape of Northwest Wales,' which includes six sites – former quarries, quarry owners' houses, quarry workers' villages, and former railway lines – that now preserve the history of the slate industry.

Dinorwig served as the backdrop for several battle sequences in the film, and also as the location of Nockmaar Castle, the seat of Queen Bavmorda. *Willow* is the first, but by no means last, entry into this collection that makes use of Wales' remarkable landscapes as the backdrop for a fantasy setting. In fact, *House of the Dragon* – the sequel series to the wildly popular *Game of Thrones* – used the exact same quarry, with its dramatic and imposing slate shelves, as the setting for their own formidable Harrenhal Castle.

Below: Waste from the quarrymen's work

Opposite: Abandoned machinery

The Hitchhiker's Guide to the Galaxy (2005)

DIRECTOR: GARTH JENNINGS
WRITERS: SCREENPLAY BY DOUGLAS ADAMS AND KAREY KIRKPATRICK, BASED ON THE BOOKS BY DOUGLAS ADAMS
STARRING: SAM ROCKWELL, MOS DEF, ZOOEY DESCHANEL, MARTIN FREEMAN, BILL NIGHY, ANNA CHANCELLOR, JOHN MALKOVICH
FILMED IN: BLAENAU GWENT
LOCATION: TREFIL QUARRY

ABOUT THE FILM

Based on the cult sci-fi books and radio series, *The Hitchhiker's Guide to the Galaxy* follows the hapless Arthur Dent (Martin Freeman) after he becomes the last human man in the universe following the demolition of Earth to build a hyperspace bypass. He is joined by his best friend and under-cover alien Ford Prefect (Yasiin Bey as Mos Def), Ford's semi-half-cousin, President of the Galaxy, and inventor of the Pan Galactic Gargle Blaster

Zaphod Beeblebrox (Sam Rockwell). Together with a miserable robot named Marvin the Paranoid Android, voiced by Alan Rickman, and the last surviving human woman Trillian Marie (Zooey Deschanel), they try to find the answer to life, the universe and everything. "If you want to survive out here, you've got to know where your towel is."

ABOUT THE LOCATION

Trefil Quarry, located just outside the village of the same name (which happens to be the highest village in Wales, at an elevation of 409 metres above sea level), was mined for limestone in the eighteenth century, leaving an eerie, crater-pocked landscape. Hidden inside the remaining rocks are the fossilised remains of a Carboniferous coral reef.

The Hitchhiker's Guide to the Galaxy premiered the same year that *Doctor Who* was revived on television screens and beat the TARDIS inhabitants to it when it came to using Trefil Quarry as an alien landscape. Trefil would become the home of the Ood in a 2008 *Doctor Who* episode starring David Tennant, but first it was the planet Vogosphere, home to a race of bureaucratic aliens known as the Vogons, who happen to be particularly terrible poets.

"The production team were looking for something truly otherworldly, and they found it at Ystrad Quarry near Trefil. They were captivated by the landscape and the atmosphere and it far exceeded their expectations. The shoot brought a real buzz to the area, with local business, from hotels to heavy equipment suppliers, benefiting directly. It was the most ambitious project that the Wales Screen Commission had assisted at that time, and it was a fantastic showcase for what the region had to offer."

— PENNY SKUSE,
Wales Screen Commission

Below & overleaf:
The alien landscape of Trefil Quarry

Harry Potter and the Deathly Hallows (Parts I and II) (2010, 2011)

DIRECTOR: DAVID YATES
WRITER: STEVE KLOVES (BASED ON NOVELS BY J.K. ROWLING)
STARRING: DANIEL RADCLIFFE, EMMA WATSON, RUPERT GRINT
FILMED IN: PEMBROKESHIRE
LOCATION: FRESHWATER WEST

ABOUT THE FILM

Of the many blockbusters that feature a snippet of Wales, the final two instalments of the *Harry Potter* franchise – Parts I and II of *The Deathly Hallows* – may have had the longest-lasting impact on the location in question. In 2009 film crews took over the spectacular Freshwater West beach in Pembrokeshire for a handful of weeks and built 'Shell Cottage', the home of main character Ron Weasley's older brother, Bill, and his wife, Fleur. The couple receive an unexpected visit from Ron, Harry and Hermione at the very end of Part I of *The Deathly Hallows*, and Part II opens with the characters still there, recuperating from a dramatic escape from Malfoy Manor and mourning the death of Dobby the House Elf.

While the Shell Cottage structure was taken down after filming, fans still visit the beach to see where it once stood, and to pay respects to Dobby's 'grave'.

Opposite & above: Shell Cottage in various states of construction, taken by Illtud Llyr Dunsford

Overleaf: Freshwater West from above

ABOUT THE LOCATION

Often described as a 'surfers' paradise' (with the caveat that only experienced swimmers should take a dip due to strong currents), Freshwater West combines sand dunes and rocky cliffs with a wide, sand-and-pebble beach to be one of the most popular locations in Pembrokeshire for locals and tourists alike. *Harry Potter* is not the only film to feature the beach on screen; 2010's *Robin Hood* and 2015's *Their Finest* were also filmed here.

"Filming at Freshwater West in Pembrokeshire is one of the more memorable locations from the *Harry Potter* back catalogue. From its vast beauty across both sea and sand dunes to its unique, west-facing position, we knew this location would provide the creative and cinematic qualities the much-loved book adaptations deserved.

"Shell Cottage is described in the books as a 'lonely and beautiful place'. Our Production Designer, Stuart Craig, briefed us with finding an expansive beach peppered with sand dunes that looked out towards a limitless sea. There are several areas of the UK that could suit this brief but, when making the final decision, it ultimately came down to the singular way in which the sun back-lit the location throughout the day. This constant source of light enabled us to shoot consistently throughout the shoot days whilst giving an other-worldly lighting effect to each scene.

"Of course, when scouting for isolated locations such as this, we must also consider how to service them. Bringing film infrastructure to intrinsically remote locations is one of the biggest challenges of our work, but also one of its greatest rewards. We spent two weeks building our 'village,' a week filming on location, and then a further two weeks returning the area to how we found it. We worked with local farmers to rent their land for our base, trucks and trailers and were in constant communication with the local National Trust team, who were very supportive of our filming. As well as hard graft, we made time to kick a football around on the beach and enjoyed meeting all the local dogs and dog owners who showed interest whilst on their daily beach walks.

"We are aware that, in the sixteen years since our filming, Freshwater West has become a landmark on the Harry Potter fan club pilgrimage. Whether it's 'mourners' laying socks in respect of Dobby or friends acting out wizarding fight scenes, we are touched that the memory of our *Harry Potter* filming lives on at this striking location. We are very grateful to the Pembrokeshire coastline for offering such a remarkable and timeless location."

— SUE QUINN,
Location Manager for *Harry Potter*

(Both images) - Behind-the-scenes courtesy of Illtud Llyr Dunsford

Overleaf: The 'muggle' approach to the beach

Snow White & the Huntsman (2012)

DIRECTOR: RUPERT SANDERS
WRITERS: EVAN DAUGHERTY, JOHN LEE HANCOCK, HOSSEIN AMINI
STARRING: KRISTEN STEWART, CHRIS HEMSWORTH, CHARLIZE THERON
FILMED IN: PEMBROKESHIRE
LOCATION: MARLOES SANDS

ABOUT THE FILM

A fairytale retelling with a twist, *Snow White & the Huntsman* stars Kristen Stewart in her first post-*Twilight* role as the titular princess. As in the original tale, Snow White's stepmother (the powerful sorceress Ravenna, played by Charlize Theron) feels threatened by Snow White and, after the young girl runs away, sends a huntsman after her with the instruction to return with her heart. Unlike in the original tale, Ravenna has murdered Snow White's father, the king, and her magic mirror has warned her that Snow White is destined to defeat her – unless, of course, Ravenna can eat Snow's heart, which will grant her immortality.

The huntsman that she employs, Eric (Chris Hemsworth), changes sides when he realises that Ravenna cannot give him what she promised in exchange for Snow White's heart, and the two band together to raise an army to rebel against the evil queen – riding across a beach to lay siege to her castle.

ABOUT THE LOCATION

Along the coast from *Harry Potter*'s Freshwater West, Marloes Sands is another dramatic Pembrokeshire beach. Identifiable by its distinctive geology (it is popular with fossil hunters), the beach makes sense as a backdrop for an epic fantasy battle, with jagged spikes of rock breaking up the expanses of sand that appear when the tide is out.

Opposite & above: Kristen Stewart and Chris Hemsworth on set, taken by Penny Skuse

Overleaf: The rocky outcrops at Marloes Sands

Snow White & the Huntsman was not Marloes' first brush with Hollywood; it was also a location for the 1968 film *The Lion in Winter*, a historical drama about Henry II and Eleanor of Aquitaine starring Peter O'Toole and Katherine Hepburn.

At the western end of the beach, accessible by a scramble over a crag of rocks, is Albion Sands – a smaller beach named after a paddle steamer which ran aground in 1837, apparently releasing four hundred pigs and a year's worth of whiskey into Pembrokeshire. The ship's prop shaft is visible at low tide. In the same direction is Gateholm, a small island overlooking Marloes Sands, upon which an Iron Age fort has been found.

"The Wales Screen Commission was able to support *Snow White & the Huntsman* when they decamped to Marloes Sands for a couple of weeks in September 2011, by providing local contacts and helping the production run smoothly. I'll never forget standing on that beach, watching Chris Hemsworth lead a cavalry charge with all the extras on horseback, thundering across the sand. For a few days, Hollywood had come to west Wales – and I had a front-row seat."

— PENNY SKUSE,
Wales Screen Commission

Below & opposite: Behind-the-scenes of the battle being filmed, taken by Penny Skuse

Overleaf: Marloes Sands

Batman: The Dark Knight Rises (2012)

DIRECTOR: CHRISTOPHER NOLAN
WRITERS: JONATHAN NOLAN, CHRISTOPHER NOLAN, DAVID S. GOYER
STARRING: CHRISTIAN BALE, TOM HARDY, ANNE HATHAWAY, JOSEPH GORDON-LEVITT
FILMED IN: SOUTH WALES
LOCATION: HENRHYD FALLS, NATIONAL TRUST PROPERTY

ABOUT THE FILM

The conclusion to Chrisopher Nolan's Batman trilogy, *The Dark Knight Rises* picks up eight years after the events of 2008's *The Dark Knight.* The interim has been quiet for Gotham with law enforcement having been granted new powers, drastically reducing the city's high levels of crime and leaving no need for the caped crusader. In the absence of his alter-ego and still processing the events of previous films in the trilogy, billionaire playboy Bruce Wayne (Christian Bale) has become reclusive. Until, that is, masked villain Bane (Tom Hardy) attacks the Gotham Stock Exchange, bankrupting Bruce and reigniting the need to don his cape and hood again as the hero that Gotham deserves.

Filming in Wales was something of a homecoming for Christian Bale, who was born and lived in Haverfordwest until the age of two.

ABOUT THE LOCATION

Henrhyd Falls, part of the Nant Llech river valley, was used as the exterior for the secret entrance to the Batcave. The tallest waterfall in south Wales with a dramatic drop of 90 feet, the falls are a popular visiting spot, due in part to the legacy of the film. The lip of the waterfall, and the bed of rock it belongs to, was known to miners in the area as 'Farewell Rock' because there was little chance of finding coal or iron beneath the sandstone.

While there may not be a secret hideaway full of bat-themed gadgets behind the falls, there is a pathway, so you too can look out for your enemies from behind a wall of rushing water.

Opposite: Henrhyd Falls by Nilfanion

"The film crew couldn't risk [the waterfall] looking anything other than a mini Niagara Falls. It was agreed to allow them to partially dam the river for several days in order to build up a reservoir of water to unleash as the camera rolled. The National Trust worked with the Environment Agency and the Countryside Council for Wales to manage any environmental impact. It was judged to be no different from having a wet spell in the summer, hardly un-heard of in Wales."

— from *National Trust on Screen* by LAUREN TAYLOR and HARVEY EDGINGTON, quoted with permission

The Graig Lech ('rocky' or 'stony' cliff) Woods, in which the waterfall can be found, have been designated as a Site of Special Scientific Interest due to a plethora of mosses, lichen, and other damp-loving plants that live there.

Above & opposite: Behind the waterfall
Opposite by Ray Bilcliff

James Bond (based on books by Ian Fleming)

From Russia With Love (1963)

DIRECTOR: TERENCE YOUNG
WRITERS: RICHARD MAIBAUM, JOHANNA HARWOOD
STARRING: SEAN CONNERY, DANIELA BIANCHI
LOCATION: YR WYDDFA (MOUNT SNOWDON) (ERYRI NATIONAL PARK)

The World Is Not Enough (1999)

DIRECTOR: MICHAEL APTED
WRITERS: NEAL PURVIS, ROBERT WADE, BRUCE FEIRSTEIN
STARRING: PIERCE BROSNAN, SOPHIE MARCEAU, ROBERT CARLYLE
LOCATION: ERYRI NATIONAL PARK

Die Another Day (2002)

DIRECTOR: LEE TAMAHORI
WRITERS: NEAL PURVIS, ROBERT WADE
STARRING: PIERCE BROSNAN, HALLE BERRY, ROSAMUND PIKE
LOCATION: PENBRYN BEACH, CEREDIGION

Quantum of Solace (2008)

DIRECTOR: MARC FORSTER
WRITERS: PAUL HAGGIS, NEAL PURVIS, ROBERT WADE
STARRING: DANIEL CRAIG, OLGA KURYLENKO, MATHIEU AMALRIC
LOCATION: LLYN PERIS (ERYRI NATIONAL PARK)

ABOUT THE FILMS

Scot Sean Connery might have been the first actor to play our favourite martini-drinking spy but who could forget Welshman Timothy Dalton's take on the role, or Cardiff-born Shirley Bassey's theme songs for *Goldfinger* (1964), *Diamonds Are Forever* (1971), and *Moonraker* (1979)? In addition to music and actors, several Bond films have used the filming locations of Wales over a number of decades. From the setting for a romantic getaway with Tatania Romanov in *From Russia With Love*; an oil pipeline in Azerbaijan in *The World is Not Enough* and the perfect lake to speedboat across in *Quantum of Solace*... 007 has been all over Eryri National Park. Meanwhile, the final scene of *Die Another Day* features a sleek, black helicopter parked next to an idyllic hut overlooking Penbryn Beach – while, inside, Pierce Brosnan's Bond pours diamonds over Halle Berry's Jinx…

Below & overleaf: Around Eryri National Park

ABOUT THE LOCATION

Designated as a National Park in 1951 and officially renamed from the English 'Snowdonia' to the original Welsh 'Eryri' in 2022, the Eryri National Park (Parc Cenedlaethol Eryri) covers 823 square miles of north Wales, encompassing nine mountain ranges, twenty-three miles of coastline, eleven thousand hectares of native woodland, five castles and an abbey.

Yr Wyddfa (Mount Snowdon) is Eryri's tallest and most popular mountain, with an elevation of 1,085 metres, making it the highest mountain in Wales. The slopes of the mountain were used to stand in for Azerbaijan in *The World is Not Enough*, with nearby hydroelectric power station Cwm Dyli being filmed as the exterior for a much-disputed oil pipeline.

Above & opposite: Llyn Peris

In *Quantum of Solace*, Bond's speedboat races across the surface of Llyn Peris, a lake that sits between the mountain Elidir Fawr and Dinorwig Quarry, where *Willow* was filmed. In fact, the lake and the quarry are closely linked, with the quarry now the site for another hydroelectric power plant and the lake serving as its reservoir.

Penbryn Beach is in a secluded cove along the Wales Coast Path and is designated as a Dark Skies Discovery Site. Considering it is also a hotspot for seal and dolphin spotting, you can understand why it would make the perfect post-mission rendezvous spot.

TELEVISION

"I'm not sure we'd be having this conversation without Julie [Gardner] and the wider range of people like Russell T [Davies] and Edward Thomas…

"Look at the diversity of *Doctor Who*. Every week you're on a spaceship, a different planet; you're in a period show, you're in a cowboy town. We could do it all in Wales, because we have such a diverse range of locations."

— GARETH SKELDING, LOCATION MANAGER FOR *DOCTOR WHO* AND OTHER PRODUCTIONS

Inside one of Cardiff's arcades

The history of television filming in Wales seems to be split very cleanly into two halves: before *Doctor Who*, and after *Doctor Who*. The show's 2005 revival, helmed by (Welsh) showrunner/writer Russell T Davies, is credited by many within the industry as having heralded a new age for Welsh TV and Filmmaking. Then-Head of Drama for BBC Wales Julie Gardner brought the show to BBC Cardiff, and from its success sprang a number of successful spin-offs – *Torchwood* and *The Sarah Jane Adventures* – all also filmed in Wales.

This seems to have opened the floodgates for other productions to film here, from BBC properties like *Merlin*, *Sherlock*, and *Da Vinci's Demons* to shows like Sky's *A Discovery of Witches* and Netflix's *Sex Education*. Now, the TV industry is thriving, with new studios like Bad Wolf and Dragon Studios established to meet demand.

In this section we explore just a few of the many TV shows that have been shot in Wales as a result of an ever-growing industry, and we celebrate the comradery that exists within it.

The Prisoner (1967–68)

CREATOR: PATRICK MCGOOHAN
STARRING: PATRICK MCGOOHAN, ANGELO MUSCAT, PETER SWANWICK
FILMED IN: NORTH WALES
LOCATION: PORTMEIRION

ABOUT THE SHOW

Of all the shows shot in Wales during the 20th century, 1960s cult classic *The Prisoner* probably had the most international fame, influencing numerous sci-fi shows and films that came after it, including *Lost, The Matrix* and *The Truman Show.* Known for its surreal, Kafkaesque setting (later parodied in Season 12 of *The Simpsons*, solidifying its cultural impact amongst a new generation), *The Prisoner* followed a former British spy known only as Number Six (Patrick McGoohan). Imprisoned in 'the Village': an idyllic but sinister closed-off community, populated by a mixture of inmates and guards, Six must figure out what his captors want, which is basically information, information, information – by hook or by crook.

Opposite & overleaf: Portmeirion

Below: 'The Prisoner' plaque at Portmeirion

Opposite: *The Prisoner* convention in Portmeirion (Marc Christiansen)

ABOUT THE LOCATION

Built by Welsh architect Clough Williams-Ellis from the bones of the former Aber Iâ estate over the course of fifty years from 1925 to 1976, Portmeirion is a whimsical, pastel-coloured folly of a village that – while pre-dating the first theme park – wouldn't look out of place at Disneyland. Inspired by Italian villages and showcasing a variety of architectural styles from Palladian to Arts and Crafts, there is something distinctively surreal about visiting Portmeirion – especially if you happen to be there during the annual convention for *The Prisoner*, in which fans dress up as the characters, have an election parade, and play human chess.

"It was in 1959 that Patrick McGoohan first visited Portmeirion, and, in a 1984 interview, recalled thinking "Here was a base for our man in isolation", indicating he had the concept of *The Prisoner* already in his mind, and identifying Portmeirion as his ideal location. Given Sir Lew Grade's blessing in September 1966, location filming took place in Sir Clough's Village, and the series was screened a year later. For those who admired the series, uniquely, we could visit what was a real film set, and recreate the iconic scenes from the series. *The Prisoner* and Portmeirion were made for each other, a marriage made in Heaven. Their relationship intertwined. Serendipity. Portmeirion helped give the series longevity; filmed elsewhere it may not have attracted the legions of fans that continue to gather each year for our annual 'pilgrimage', a celebration and our convention.

— DAVID BARRIE,
founding member of Six of One,
The Prisoner Appreciation Society.

Doctor Who (2005 onwards)

SHOWRUNNERS: RUSSELL T DAVIES, STEVEN MOFFAT, CHRIS CHIBNALL
STARRING: CHRISTOPHER ECCLESTON, DAVID TENNANT, MATT SMITH, PETER CAPALDI, JODIE WHITTAKER, NCUTI GATWA, BILLIE PIPER
FILMED: ACROSS WALES, PRIMARILY THE SOUTH.

ABOUT THE SHOW

Britain's favourite sci-fi show about a Time Lord and a little blue box is possibly the first project that comes to mind when most people think about filming in Wales. For those unfamiliar with The Doctor, he (and, more recently, she) is an ageless two-hearted alien with a soft spot for saving planet Earth from a variety of extraterrestrial threats, often on Christmas Day. The Doctor and their companion-of-the-moment travel through time and space, sometimes visiting the past or future of Earth, other times taking trips to other planets or ships throughout the universe. The original series ran from 1963 to 1989; it was revived in 2005 and filmed in the BBC Cymru studios in Cardiff Bay.

ABOUT THE LOCATION

We could fill a whole book just listing the places in Wales that *Doctor Who* has filmed over the last 20 years. The TARDIS and its inhabitants have been everywhere from Cardiff city centre to the sand dunes of Merthyr Mawr; from the historical halls of Tredegar House and Cardiff Castle to the National Botanic Garden of Wales and back again, with a few dozen trips in between. It could be argued that Wales has been the most versatile actor in the series, playing not only various countries across the world, but also planets across the universe.

"The great thing about alien planets is that very few people have visited any so the creativity has no boundaries – however, the budgetary side of things does, so it was an ongoing process to decide what should be a set and what should be a location, and indeed how very often both sets and locations would marry to create a world…

"Closing the Severn bridge and the Bute Tunnels on separate occasions, landing and manoeuvring jumbo jet planes at the British Airways factory at Cardiff Airport and seeing the Dalek in the depths of the Millennium Stadium, the home of Welsh rugby, are all standout moments and just go to show how much all the film production in Wales [is] valued by the authorities. It also is testimony to how amazing our location managers are, as without them none of these worlds would exist."

— EDWARD THOMAS,
Production Manager
for *Doctor Who, Torchwood,*
The Sarah Jane Adventures and more

Above: Filming in Cardiff Bay, taken by Penny Skuse

Opposite & overleaf: Inside the Cardiff arcades, used in the Series 9 episode 'Face the Raven' as secret London streets.

MORGAN
QUARTER
HOT FOOD
GOWER
CRUMBS
KITCHEN
EXTRA
SEATING
Available
UP
STAIRS

For the 2007 Christmas special, 'Voyage of the Damned', a former industrial building in Swansea became the ballroom of a Titanic-themed spaceship on which Astrid Peth (played by the episode's guest star Kylie Minogue) works as a maid. Evidently, the costume department were a little too good at their job for this episode:

"Now, you take Kylie Minogue in a maid's outfit to Swansea for the day, and you shoot in the old Swansea Exchange building just along from Morgans Hotel. And we've got a little green room in Morgans Hotel. So Kylie wanders back, as you do, past the hotel, and there's two little old ladies sat outside having a cream tea and a coffee. They spotted Kylie – or, spotted a lady in a waitress outfit – and said 'Oh, dear, you couldn't get us two more coffees could you please?' She said, 'Of course.' And they had no idea who she was, and to this day, I don't think they know who she was. And in she went, came back with two coffees, two scones, left them on the table; said 'There you go, ladies' and paid for them herself.

"That's the sort of thing that I want, from putting a massive film crew and disrupting areas, I want a bit of payback to the public and nice stories like that. And we do, we get that, and it's really heartwarming. And when you've got somebody like that, who buys into it, then, you know, it makes it all worthwhile."

— GARETH SKELDING,
Location Manager

The TARDIS at Rhossili – taken by Penny Skuse

Torchwood (2006–2008)

SHOWRUNNERS: RUSSELL T DAVIES, CHRIS CHIBNALL
STARRING: JOHN BARROWMAN, EVE MYLES, GARETH DAVID-LLOYD
FILMED IN: SOUTH WALES
LOCATIONS: CARDIFF BAY

ABOUT THE SHOW

Torchwood was created as a spinoff from *Doctor Who*, catering to the show's adult audience and incorporating more mature and less 'family-friendly' themes into its plotlines. The series follows the Torchwood Institute, a group of agents led by *Doctor Who* character Captain Jack Harkness (John Barrowman), who investigate Earth-bound incidents involving aliens. The audience meets the team – including Ianto Jones (Gareth David-Lloyd), Owen Harper (Burn Gorman), and Toshiko Sato (Indira Varma) – via Gwen Cooper (Eve Myles), the team's newest recruit.

Unlike its parent show, where Wales was often used as a stand-in for other locations, *Torchwood* was set very specifically in Cardiff, citing a local rift in the spacetime continuum as the reason for an uplift in alien-based mysteries in the area. The secret entrance to the team's HQ was on the boardwalk of Mermaid Quay, beneath Roald Dahl Plass.

The entrance is somewhat less secret today, however, as it has become known as 'Ianto's Shrine', and hundreds of fans of the show visit annually to leave fan art, flowers, and other mementos in memory of one of the show's most beloved characters.

"The Ianto Shrine is a great thing. And it's a very small part of the wider picture of Cardiff Bay, Cardiff and that sort of thing. There are many other locations that are very well renowned, but they're privately owned, so we don't really want to publicise where they all are. My favourite ever episode of *Doctor Who* was 'Blink,' written by Stephen Moffat, with the stone angels. The brief was: "Find Scooby Doo's house on a hill." So that was a house in Newport. People live in it. So we don't really want to publicise too much where they are, for the privacy of these people who are going about their daily life. [So] having an outdoor site [like the Shrine] is great – people can go somewhere public, and celebrate what's been achieved there, and, you know, the bigger picture of what's been achieved in Wales."

— GARETH SKELDING,
Location Manager

Opposite: Filming at the boardwalk in Cardiff Bay – taken by Penny Skuse

Overleaf: The Pierhead Building, Millennium Centre, and Senedd making up the skyline in Cardiff Bay

BYWYD
LLAWN

Tamaid

ABOUT THE LOCATION

Cardiff Bay, formerly known as 'Tiger Bay,' was once one of the busiest ports in the world. Indeed, it was the site of the first million-pound deal, exporting coal from the Welsh coalfields across the globe. As a result of this, the area became Wales' oldest and largest multi-ethnic community. It was also the birthplace of one of Wales' most famous singers – Dame Shirley Bassey. The Norwegian Church where Llandaff-born Roald Dahl was christened can still be visited today.

Cardiff Bay went under massive regeneration during the 1990s and 2000s, transforming the historic dockland into an ambitious waterfront development including a freshwater lake with a barrage, the Senedd (Welsh Parliament), the Wales Millennium Centre, an Olympic Swimming Pool built for the 2012 Olympics, and a lively waterside bar and restaurant scene.

On the contrast between shooting Cardiff for London in *Doctor Who* and shooting Cardiff for itself in *Torchwood*, Edward Thomas said:

"Shooting Cardiff for Cardiff was, of course, the easy part in the beginning. [It] got a little more challenging, as with the success of the show growing, so did the fan base. We regularly found ourselves being followed by well-wishers and fans."

"[A particularly fond memory is] the moment we launched a missile at the wonderful Eve Miles's character Gwen from a Black Hawk Helicopter hovering over the beautiful beach of Rhossili straight into the Rectory National Trust property perched on the hillside... because that's what it said on the page."

— EDWARD THOMAS,
Production Designer

Opposite top: Filming by the Pierhead Building in Cardiff Bay, courtesy of Penny Skuse.

Opposite bottom: A fan-built shrine for the character Ianto now marks where the entrance to Torchwood HQ was filmed.

IANTO'S SHRINE
Happy Birthday
Happy Birthday
Happy Birthday

Gavin & Stacey (2007–2024)

SHOWRUNNERS AND WRITERS: RUTH JONES, JAMES CORDEN
STARRING: MATTHEW HORNE, JOANNA PAGE, RUTH JONES, JAMES CORDEN
FILMED IN: SOUTH WALES
LOCATIONS: TRINITY STREET (BARRY), BARRY ISLAND, DINAS POWYS

ABOUT THE SHOW

One of the BBC's biggest shows of the 2000s, *Gavin & Stacey* is a rom-com/sit-com with a surprisingly heartwarming twist. It tells the story of star-crossed lovers Gavin (based in Essex) and Stacey (from Barry) – who meet through work and overcome distance, family drama, and cultural differences to end up together.

Originally airing between 2007-2010, the show captured the hearts of the UK, and returned in both 2019 and 2024 with primetime Christmas specials to resolve the secondary love story between Nessa (Ruth Jones) and Smithy (James Corden).

This is another show that has left a mark on its location; visitors to Barry Island (affectionately known as Barrybados to locals) can take photos with a photo wall of the cast, visit Nessa's arcade, and take *Gavin & Stacey* themed tours. Tidy.

ABOUT THE LOCATION

Gavin & Stacey was filmed in various places across south Wales (Pam and Mick's house, for example, is actually in Dinas Powys, not Essex), but none stuck in the public mind as much as Barry Island. A peninsula connected to Barry 'proper' by docks built in the 1880s, the Island was a popular Victorian seaside resort, now featuring a Pleasure Park, colourful beach huts, and the distinctive Western and Eastern shelters – two covered areas built in the classical style along the promenade overlooking the beach. These can be seen in many shots in the show. Marco's Cafe, the bright blue coffee shop where Stacey works in series three, is still open and is popular with fans making a pilgrimage.

Opposite: Gavin & Stacey have made their mark on Barry Island

Welcome to...
Island Leisure
Where GAVIN & STACEY is filmed

CHANGE
NESSA'S SLOTS
BARRY ISLAND
OH MY CHRIS
SUGAR TITS
OH! WHAT'S OCCURRIN'
BARRY ISLAND'S CRACKIN'
I ♥ GAVIN & STACEY
"Tidy"

The cast and creators of the show have spoken often about the feeling of community in Barry, and especially the connection that locals felt with the show, that made *Gavin & Stacey* special. It even inspired other television makers. Midge Ferguson, Location Manager for *Sex Education* told us that inciting that feeling of ownership was something he aimed for: "That's something I wanted to do, like they did with *Gavin & Stacey.* It's 'their' show."

"Since *Gavin & Stacey* first aired in May 2007, it has captured the hearts of viewers across the world. While audiences were drawn in by the love stories at the heart of the show, Barry Island – so often the backdrop to those stories – became an unexpected star in its own right.

"Fans have flocked here from the very beginning to walk in the footsteps of their favourite characters, and that excitement has only grown. Following the announcement of 'The Finale' in May 2024, visitor numbers reached record highs as people came to celebrate the place they know and love from the screen.

"The show is equally important to local people, who have embraced *Gavin & Stacey* with pride and joy, welcoming visitors eager to share in the magic of Barry Island.

The impact has been nothing short of phenomenal. Local businesses report bumper years thanks to *Gavin & Stacey*, and the year-round draw of the show has extended the visitor season well beyond the summer months.

"*Gavin & Stacey* has truly catapulted Barry Island into the hearts and homes of millions, and we are incredibly grateful for the positive legacy it has brought to our traditional seaside resort in Wales."

— NIA HOLLINS,
Principal Tourism & Marketing Officer,
Vale of Glamorgan Council

Opposite, above & overleaf: A sunny day on Barry Island

Sherlock (2010–2017)

CREATED BY: MARK GATISS, STEVEN MOFFAT
BASED ON BOOKS BY ARTHUR CONAN DOYLE
STARRING: BENEDICT CUMBERBATCH, MARTIN FREEMAN, UNA STUBBS
FILMED IN: SOUTH WALES
LOCATIONS: CARDIFF, NEWPORT, SWANSEA

ABOUT THE SHOW

Created by *Doctor Who* showrunner Steven Moffat and fellow *Doctor Who* writer Mark Gatiss (who went on to play Mycroft Holmes in the series), *Sherlock* was a modernised retelling of Arthur Conan Doyle's classic detective stories. Starring Benedict Cumberbatch in the titular role and Martin Freeman as his not-so-bumbling side-kick John Watson, the series ran for four seasons, each comprising three 90-minute episodes. The programme's plots were initially based on books by Arthur Conan Doyle, though the fourth season deviated from this somewhat. Updating the books to the modern-day, with technology to match, Sherlock employs state-of-the-art forensics and a twenty-first-century understanding of science to find clues and make connections; while Watson writes a blog rather than stories for *The Strand Magazine*.

ABOUT THE LOCATION

Although Sherlock Holmes is one of London's most famous fictional residents, and his iconic address of 221B Baker Street remained sacrosanct in the series, Sherlock's London would be shot primarily in south Wales cities. Many of the buildings along and around Museum Avenue in Cardiff – including the National Museum of Wales, Cardiff's City Hall (with the distinctive dragon on the roof carefully cropped away) and a number of Cardiff University buildings – were used to replicate London's columned Edwardian architecture. The halls of Sherlock's 'mind palace' were filmed inside some of these buildings, too. Interiors of The Temple of Peace, a ten-minute walk away from the Civic Centre, was also used in the episode, 'The Blind Banker'.

Opposite: Benedict Cumberbatch as Sherlock and Martin Freeman as Watson on the steps of the National Museum in Cardiff

AMGUEDDFA GENEDLAETHOL CYMRU

"Recreating London in Cardiff, Swansea and Newport was always a challenge as the scale of the roads and landmarks differ considerably. We knew we would need to visit London from time to time but then retreat to Wales to fill in the gaps. Fans from all of the shows will certainly see a crossover in terms of locations used, but you just have to believe you have done enough to not take the viewer out of the narrative with your decision making. For example – in the case of *Doctor Who* I decided that all the bin bags in London would be red. A small but successful motif to subliminally remind the audience where we are while injecting some colour into the frame.

"Shooting in Cardiff compared to London in the early days was far easier technically, for sure. The price tag attached to both cities varied considerably, with Cardiff being less expensive. However due to the amount of filming that now takes place in and around Cardiff it would be interesting to see if that has changed. Locations, unit bases and warehouse space all come with a price tag and rateable value which influences the money left for the on-screen ambition."

— EDWARD THOMAS,
Production Manager

"I suppose 85% of [*Sherlock*] was shot in Wales. So you go to London and do your big wow, running along the Thames past the London Eye… then you turn left, near an alley in Newport. So that's the clever thing of how we can join these things together with it, with the very talented crews we've got here in Wales… It's just how you cleverly stitch it together."

— GARETH SKELDING,
Location Manager

Above: Filming inside the Temple of Peace, Cardiff (Hartswood films)

Opposite: The entrance to the Museum

Da Vinci's Demons (2013–2015)

CREATED BY: DAVID S. GOYER
STARRING: TOM RILEY, GREGG CHILINGIRIAN, EROS VLAHOS
FILMED IN: SOUTH WALES
LOCATIONS: SWANSEA, NEATH, PORT TALBOT, ABERGLASNEY HOUSE AND GARDENS, MARGAM CASTLE, CASTELL COCH

ABOUT THE SHOW

Da Vinci's Demons reimagines the younger years of Leonardo da Vinci (Tom Riley). The show takes inspiration from what we know of da Vinci's life, while adding a pinch or two of poetic licence. Embroiled within a political vipers' nest, the brilliant young artist navigates the patronage, politics and schemes of the Medici and Pazzi families in fifteenth-century Florence, while working on his art, inventions, and investigating a Mithraic cult or two. Da Vinci's genius is the driving force of the show, as he navigates one mystery after another using only his wit.

ABOUT THE LOCATION

Alien planets aside, Renaissance Italy may be one of the harder orders when it comes to transforming Wales for the screen. The weather, for one thing, is famously different.

"On *Da Vinci's Demons,* the challenges of recreating Italy, Constantinople, and so much more, were massive. From the off, I knew we had to find a studio space large enough to facilitate what [would] be huge sets, from Vatican interiors to the streets of Florence, Rome and Otranto, to name a few. I wanted to create sets that were physically linked, allowing the cast to go on journeys in camera, to accentuate the scale of the world.

Margam Castle would provide us with many of the interiors of the Medici palace and the amazing landscape that surrounds it; along with the Gower Peninsula, paired with Bay Studios a few miles down the road. [These] provided the perfect solution to think big and give the show a scale it deserved."

— EDWARD THOMAS,
Production Designer

Margam Castle from above (Clément Proust)

Margam Castle in Margam, Port Talbot, is a nineteenth-century Tudor Gothic mansion designed by the architect Thomas Hopper for the Talbot family. A fire in 1977 destroyed much of the interior, and restoration works have been taking place ever since. Today, Margam Castle and the country park surrounding it are open to visitors, and home to a herd of around three hundred deer, as well as fourteen of the eighteen species of bat native to the United Kingdom. The Grade I listed gardens are home to a historic Fern-leaved Beech which won Wales Tree of the Year 2020.

While Da Vinci may not have ever actually visited Margam Park, it has had its fair share of famous inhabitants, including one who didn't become well-known until after his death. Robert Scott, a former gamekeeper at the castle, has been spotted on the grounds and staircase of the house, and was even the star of his own TV show – an episode of the American paranormal investigation show *Ghost Hunters* in 2010.

Below: Margam Castle

Opposite top: Castell Coch

Opposite bottom: Neath Abbey

A Discovery of Witches (2018–2022)

SHOWRUNNER: KATE BROOKE
BASED ON BOOKS BY DEBORAH HARKNESS
STARRING: MATTHEW GOODE, TERESA PALMER, ALEX KINGSTON
FILMED IN: SOUTH WEST WALES
LOCATIONS: ABERGLASNEY GARDENS (CARMARTHENSHIRE),
CAREW CASTLE (PEMBROKESHIRE), LLYN Y FAN FACH (CARMARTHENSHIRE), CARDIFF MARKET,
INSOLE COURT (CARDIFF), TRETOWER COURT (CRICKHOWELL),
OXWICH AND RHOSSILI BAYS (THE GOWER PENINSULA), CAERPHILLY CASTLE

ABOUT THE SHOW

A Discovery of Witches follows Diana Bishop (Teresa Palmer), an academic and tenured professor at Oxford who has put her witchy family history behind her – until her research leads to a magical manuscript in the Bodleian Library which forces her back into the witches' world. Trying to solve the mystery of the ancient book's secrets, she joins forces with Matthew Clairmont (Matthew Goode), a charismatic vampire.

ABOUT THE LOCATION

The shooting schedule of *A Discovery of Witches* reads like a hitlist of some of the most impressive-looking Welsh castles and stately homes.

Matthew's moody study at Oxford University is actually the reading room at Insole Court, a wealthy mineowners house on the outskirts of Cardiff where the family's fortunes can be tracked via the different architectural styles added throughout the years. Sold to Cardiff Council in 1932, the house has now spent more time as a community property than as a residential home. It served as headquarters for a number of local organisations during the Second World War, and since 2010 has been owned by a local Trust. Today it is a lovely place to spend an afternoon, with well-tended gardens, a cafe, and a second-hand bookshop in the old butler's pantry.

Below: The Reading Room at Insole Court, courtesy of Lloyd Glanville

Opposite: The Gower Peninsula

"The filming boom in south Wales has provided exciting opportunities for heritage sites. There is the benefit of the location fee of course but also the interest it can generate in your venue, especially in the case of cult shows such as *Doctor Who* and *Sherlock*. It's important not to underestimate the impact the filming can have in terms of disruption and potential risk to the fabric of the building. However, by providing clear guidelines and building relationships with local crew you can ensure the building is looked after and still benefit from the increased exposure. I have seen first-hand the interest it can generate, with families visiting Cardiff, even as their only stop in the UK, specifically to view locations from their favourite TV shows.

"Often TV shows can make an improvement that is retained once filming is complete. Insole Court still has wallpaper in the old Swiss Wing that was put up for *A Discovery of Witches* and suits the period of the house, covering modern plaster."

— LLOYD GLANVILLE,
CEO of Insole Court
and former Heritage Director of
Cardiff Castle

The moat at Caerphilly Castle, which sits in the middle of Caerphilly town centre (about a ten-minute walk from The Big Cheese statue), was used as a stand-in for the Thames river in London. Caerphilly is the biggest castle in Wales, built in the thirteenth century to maintain English control over the area out of fear of Llywelyn ap Gruffudd, also known as the 'last' Prince of Wales.

Overleaf: Caerphilly Castle in the snow

His Dark Materials (2019–2022)

CREATED BY: JACK THORNE
BASED ON BOOKS BY PHILIP PULLMAN
STARRING: DAFNE KEEN, KIT CONNOR, JAMES MCAVOY, RUTH WILSON, LIN-MANUEL MIRANDA
FILMED IN: SOUTH AND WEST WALES
LOCATIONS: WOLF STUDIOS (CARDIFF), BLAENAVON IRONWORKS, BANNAU BRYCHEINIOG (BRECON BEACONS) NATIONAL PARK INCLUDING LLYN Y FAN FACH, DUNRAVEN BAY (VALE OF GLAMORGAN), ST. GOVAN'S CHAPEL (PEMBROKESHIRE), WENTWOOD FOREST (MONMOUTHSHIRE), MARGAM PARK (PORT TALBOT), PLASTURTON GARDENS AND THE RIVER SEVERN (CARDIFF), ST DONAT'S CASTLE (LLANTWIT MAJOR)

ABOUT THE SHOW

Adapted from the best-selling fantasy trilogy from the 1990s to 2000s, *His Dark Materials* tells the story of Lyra (Dafne Keen), a young ward at Jordan College in an alternative universe's Oxford. Venturing across a world almost like our own with her dæmon Pan, Lyra befriends witches, Gyptians, talking polar bears and a boy from our own world who's a very long way from home – all in a search for her missing best friend.

One of the stand-out features of the TV series was the puppetry used for the dæmons; external pieces of the human soul which manifest in animal forms in Lyra's world. Another lasting memory is the story of Lin-Manuel Miranda, creator of *Hamilton*, who played the aeronaut Lee Scoresby, who during filming in Cardiff surprised attendees at a local musical theatre karaoke night.

Opposite: Ruth Wilson as Mrs Coulter, shot at Wolf Studios Wales in Cardiff (Bad Wolf / HBO / BBC)

ABOUT THE LOCATION

As with other TV shows mentioned in this section – especially *A Discovery of Witches*, which was also set in Oxford – *His Dark Materials* needed areas in Wales to masquerade as other towns and cities in England for certain locations, especially as many of them are iconic to book readers.

"And yes, we had to go to Oxford to capture a lot of that. But we also cheated a lot of it in Wales. You know, the incredible Atlantic College in St Donat's Castle is really amazing for that. We built some great sets for those sort of shows… I mean, we were following the book, obviously, the amazing books from Philip Pullman in *His Dark Materials*, and that dragged us into sort of various ways. We just had to creep into the border a little bit, into sort of Gloucestershire and those canals and all that, for Lyra's world with the Gyptians. But... that was really cool and different and gave us a little different look. But again, it's just over that bridge for us."

— GARETH SKELDING,
Location Manager

Below: Blaenavon Ironworks was used as the backdrop for Trollesund

The locations used for *His Dark Materials* range from the industrial (Blaenavon Ironworks, used as the background for the Trollesund, the home of Iorek Byrnison the bear) to the mythological. Llyn y Fan Fach (roughly 'Lake of the Small Hill' or 'Peak'), which lies within the Bannau Brycheiniog National Park, where Lord Asriel (James McAvoy) camped out – and which was also used in *A Discovery of Witches* – features in one of the tales in the Mabinogion. It was the home of the Lady of the Lake; a beautiful fairy princess who rose from the waters and met a young farmer, whom she agreed to marry after being wooed by bread (who hasn't been there?). Her only caveat is that if he hits her three times, she will leave him. Together they had three sons, who grew up to become the Physicians of Myddfai, legendary figures in their own rights. The story ends sadly, however, when the husband is unable to keep his promise not to strike his wife, and she returns to the lake – taking with her all of their farm animals. She would rise periodically after this to teach her sons the arts of herbalism and medicine.

St Govan's Chapel, an isolated stone structure hidden amongst striking cliffs along the Pembrokeshire coast, provided the perfect hideaway for Mrs Coulter (Ruth Wilson) and her golden monkey dæmon. The myth of the chapel holds that St Govan was set upon by a gang of pirates while walking along the coast one day and as he ran away from them, the cliffs opened up to hide him. He decided to stay in the miraculous space and acquired a silver bell that he rang to warn locals whenever the pirates returned. The bell is said to now be encased in stone near the chapel, where legend says it will grant wishes to visitors.

Above: Llyn y Fan Fach, where Lord Asriel camped out

Overleaf: St Govan's Chapel, location of Mrs Coulter's hideout

Sex Education (2019–2023)

CREATED BY: LAURIE NUNN
DIRECTOR: BEN TAYLOR
STARRING: ASA BUTTERFIELD, GILLIAN ANDERSON, NCUTI GATWA, EMMA MACKEY
FILMED IN: SOUTH WALES
LOCATIONS: TINTERN, MONMOUTH AND LLANDOGO (THE WYE VALLEY), THE PAGET ROOMS AND ALL SAINTS CHURCH HALL (PENARTH), NEWPORT INTERNATIONAL SPORTS VILLAGE, CWMBRAN STADIUM, MARGAM CASTLE AND COUNTRY PARK AND MARGAM ABBEY (PORT TALBOT), CWMCARN FOREST, ST FAGANS NATIONAL HISTORY MUSEUM (CARDIFF), FORMER UNIVERSITY OF SOUTH WALES CAERLEON CAMPUS (NEWPORT)

ABOUT THE SHOW

The show's premise revolves around Otis Milburn (Asa Butterfield), son of a sex therapist (Gillian Anderson), as he uses the knowledge he's gleaned from his mother to help his fellow students with their own sexual problems and questions. Helping him in this business venture is Maeve (Emma Mackey), and by his side is his best friend Eric (Ncuti Gatwa).

Before the first season aired on Netflix to great popularity, *Sex Education* had to go by a pseudonym in order to be 'allowed' to shoot in certain places:

"It had the working title *Being Schooled* – as in, you've been taught and schooled. Because if I mentioned the word 'sex education'... no. Authorities and councils would say no. Then series one comes out. Series two, they were clambering over us to help us."

The roaring success of the show was in part due to its universal appeal, using tropes from British and American teen shows, as well as a mixture of retro and modern styling and technology, to create a world that feels familiar to audience members at any age.

"The principles were very much of Ben [Taylor]'s making that it was to be timeless and placeless. And it's because [learning about sex and coming of age] affects everybody from all generations, whatever God you worship, or anything like that. That's the premise of what it was meant to be. And then he was a massive fan, or is a massive fan, of John Hughes' work, of course."

— MIDGE FERGUSON,
Location Manager

Opposite: The River Wye

ABOUT THE LOCATIONS

Sex Education is an example of a programme that really allows Wales to display its versatility and wide variety of locations, all within a relatively small geographical area. In fact, this steered a lot of the decision-making:

"It was [originally] written about a comprehensive school in north London. And then the location was found, the old university in Caerleon [where the school was originally filmed]," explains Midge, who grew up in the Wye Valley. "[And] luckily, [Ben's] ideas, when he said to me, 'this is the kind of thing I'm after', I said, well, that's just up the road, mate. We've got those bridges, we've got those rivers, we've got these nondescript houses. We've got these things that can be iconic… the house in *Sex Education* was nothing that was described. And I found that kind of by chance, but I knew where it was because it was above a pub I used to drink in as a teenager.

"And also [Samantha Harley, the production designer] wanted the look that, again, was timeless. But you look at architecture from the last twenty, thirty, years – it's dull and boring architecture. Even the smallest of houses had interesting windows in the 70s, and so that's what we were kind of looking for, to help tell the story. And so, in a way, knowing the Wye Valley as I did, having grown up there as a teenager, it worked perfectly. I mean, it would have been a completely different show if it'd been based in north London."

— MIDGE FERGUSON,
Location Manager

Below: Outside Saint Fagans

Opposite: Monmouth from above

The Wye Valley, where the Wye crosses into both England and Wales, gives *Sex Education* its unique visuals. While the iconic hillside home of Otis and Jean (Gillian Anderson) is on the English side of the river (meaning that the majority of the beautiful view is, in fact, Wales), the towns of Tintern, Monmouth and Llandogo all played host to the show. Browns Village Stores, a corner shop frequented by the characters and employing a couple of them, is in reality Browns General Store in Llandogo, and the bridge along which Otis and Eric walk to school is the Wireworks Bridge in Tintern. In season four, when the gang's school moves to a new location, they use the Duke of Beaufort Iron Bridge in Monmouth.

The reference to the metal used to make the bridge is not irrelevant: Wye, like the rest of the Valleys, was built on mining. The production of iron, as well as copper and tin, was big business for the Wye back in the day. Now, the area's biggest industry is tourism, with the area being a must-see for visitors as far back as the eighteenth century, when a number of famous poets and artists visited to be inspired by the area's natural beauty. The medieval Tintern Abbey, which was ransacked during Henry VIII's suppression of the monasteries, is also a big draw – and while it isn't shown in *Sex Education*, in real life it looms large behind the Wireworks Bridge.

Looking across the River Wye

House of the Dragon (2022–ongoing)

CREATED BY: RYAN J. CONDAL, MIGUEL SAPOCHNIK
BASED ON BOOKS BY GEORGE R. R. MARTIN
STARRING: MATT SMITH, EMMA D'ARCY, OLIVIA COOKE
FILMED IN: NORTH WALES
LOCATIONS: ERYRI (SNOWDONIA) NATIONAL PARK, TREFOR QUARRY (GWYNEDD), DINORWIG QUARRY, OGWEN VALLEY (NANT FFRANCON), PENMON POINT, LLANDDWYN BEACH, BEAUMARIS BEACH AND THE MENAI STRAIT (ANGLESEY)

ABOUT THE SHOW

A prequel series to the blockbuster hit *Game of Thrones*, *House of the Dragon* is set roughly two centuries before the events of the first episode of *Thrones*, and explores the history and eventual decline of the House of Targaryen in the lead-up to a war known as the 'Dance of the Dragons', which is referenced in the original series.

The show revolves primarily around the tension between Rhanaenyra Targaryen (Emma D'Arcy) and Alicent Hightower (Olivia Cooke). The former is the heir apparent to the crown; the latter is Rhanaenyra's childhood friend who in adulthood becomes her stepmother.

ABOUT THE LOCATIONS

House of the Dragon, like *Willow* before it, uses the vaguely unnatural landscapes of now-disused quarries as settings for imposing castles – an easy way to let unwanted visitors know that you do not want to mess with the inhabitants. In fact, one of the quarries used by *House of the Dragon*, for the ruined and potentially cursed Harrenhal Castle, is Dinorwig – the same quarry used in the film *Willow*. Meanwhile, the Targaryen's imposing ancestral seat of Dragonstone is set at Trefor Quarry. Active from 1850 to 1963, Trefor was a source of granite – which explains the dark rock that gives Dragonstone its gothic atmosphere.

The coastline of Anglesey (Ynys Môn) has played host to a number of battle scenes. The largest island both in Wales and the Irish Sea, Anglesey is naturally well-endowed when it comes to beaches. Llanddwyn beach, where some filming took place, connects to Llanddwyn Island, which was once home to Santes Dwynwen, also known as the 'Welsh St. Valentine.' St Dwynwen, devastated that her father forbade her from marrying her true love, wished to forget him – and he was promptly turned into a block of ice. He eventually thawed out, but by the time he did, Dwynwen had moved to Llanddwyn Island, where she chose to remain unmarried and founded an abbey. Legend had it that if a pair of lovers visited a specific well on the island, two magic fish (or in some versions of the story, eels) would predict their future. If the fish swam, their love was true; if they stayed still, it was not to be.

It might be a little on the nose to say that Wales is an obvious home for a show with 'dragons' in the title, but it's more than our flag that brought Westeros to Welsh shores:

"It was great to be shooting in Wales with its stunning scenery and landscapes… I had no hesitation in taking *House of the Dragon* there... and we were blessed with the most glorious weather too"

— KEVIN DE LA NOY,
Executive Producer to the BBC

Opposite: Slate piles at Dinorwig Quarry

AFTERWORD

by Celyn Jones

So there you have it, our little cinematic odyssey of Wales, where it played its part in many a story with versatility and great aplomb. Who knew our streets, mountains, buildings and beaches could shine so brightly... yet at the same time, hide that light from the rest of the world, in fear of looking fully at ourselves?

Once the cameras pack up and the trucks leave, with no more entourages, rubber-necking autograph hunters or nimble paparazzi, we are left with just tales to tell and a film or TV show to watch as evidence. At the beginning, I talked about the production process of the film, which takes effort, belief and courage, with a dollop of stupidity from all involved. But the life cycle of a film has a long tail and its legacy is something that never fails to surprise. Making a film is a very conscious thing and we are familiar with words like vision and objective. The language has a clarity and surety about itself but the legacy.... Well, that is up to the Gods. I'm not talking about the selling and distribution of the films or the promotion or lack of promotion or endorsement, as that's a whole other book, like the dark arts. No, this is about people and place.

We cannot prepare for every honest reaction we receive... that letter of care from a person who is moved to thank you for shining a light on a world they are part of; or a section of society that deserves to be seen and highlighted in that way. How can one guess that something created might live for so long and mean so much to people at particular points in their life? How can we quantify the impressions that stories make on young people, who then grow and become adults and sometimes film people in their own right? We, in turn, become old but fulfilled that the 'thing we did years ago' added to someone else's journey.

When I first flirted with the idea of screenwriting, I shared my nerves with a director who I respected and admired. He looked at me and said, 'Everyone in the world at one point has not written a script before. You're no different so don't worry, just do it!' It freed me up. Beginnings are not exclusive to the creators either. It's an industry and each project is filled with beginnings, from the work-experience runner who goes on to produce, to the graduate who finds a fitting department and then grows into a head of department down the line and later on gives others a chance.

There are countless stories of people's first experiences on set that lead on to various careers behind the camera. We all remember our first chance and opportunity. Again, we can't prepare or factor this in on the page – it's just another little set of miracles that happen. It is lovely when you bump into people down the road in your career and you share or remember a moment when you worked together. That's why it's never goodbye, it's always 'so long' or 'until the next one'. All the while, it is important for young people who are circling the industry to know that it is viable and exciting and not just for the reckless dreamers.

For example, it feels like yesterday we made *Set Fire to the Stars* but to some people it's a cult classic they watched on repeat at film school, years ago. Everyone in these pages will have a similar anecdote. How strange and satisfying that this wild endeavour of an industry can weather

Opposite top: Llanddwyn Island and Newborough Beach

Opposite bottom: Filming of 'The Toll' in Pembrokeshire, courtesy of Andrew Ryan Hooper

the storm of criticism or success, or both, and still find green shoots for others to cling onto and be inspired by. We can't prepare for the life or legacy of any of these films but for those who birthed them, witnessed them or embraced them, we can indulge in that little extra spark and revel in the guilty pleasure that it happened and happened for us, in Wales and for everyone.

When I think of the mess and noise that we all brought to these locations for a brief moment, the whirlwind of celebrity and personality, only to leave without a trace, it reminds me of the last lines from *The Tempest*;

> 'Our revels now are ended. These our actors,
> As I foretold you, were all spirits and
> Are melted into air, into thin air...
> ... We are such stuff
> As dreams are made on, and our little life
> Is rounded with a sleep.'

So please remember that this is an industry, and Wales could well be the fire in that crucible, for all to see. It is my privilege to be a part of it all.

Celyn Jones

ACKNOWLEDGEMENTS

With special thanks to everyone who has helped us to make this book by providing quotes, photographs, and context. Especially to Penny Skuse, without whom much of this would have been impossible; Gareth Skelding and Midge Ferguson, both of whom gave their time to talk to us about television in Wales; and Ryan Andrew Hooper, who provided the beautiful cover photograph.

ABOUT THE AUTHORS

Celyn Jones is a critically acclaimed and multi-award-winning Actor, writer, producer and director from Anglesey, North Wales. He founded the internationally renowned film company Mad as Birds and is a proud Welsh ambassador for the youth charity Into Film.

Frances Turpin is a writer and publishing professional originally from Greater Manchester, now living in Cardiff. A one-time extra in a single episode of *My Parents Are Aliens* at the age of twelve, *Film & TV Places of Wales* is her return to the dazzling world of show business

Filming of 'The Toll' in Pembrokeshire, courtesy of Andrew Ryan Hooper

INDEX